D1349607

LOWER PIEDMONT COUNTRY

AMERICAN FOLKWAYS

Edited by ERSKINE CALDWELL

GOLDEN GATE COUNTRY by Gertrude Atherton

DESERT COUNTRY by Edwin Corle

DEEP DELTA COUNTRY by Harnett T. Kane

PALMETTO COUNTRY by Stetson Kennedy

NORTH STAR COUNTRY by Meridel Le Sueur

PIÑON COUNTRY by Haniel Long

SOUTHERN CALIFORNIA COUNTRY by Carey McWilliams

LOWER PIEDMONT COUNTRY by H. C. Nixon

OZARK COUNTRY by Otto Ernest Rayburn

MORMON COUNTRY by Wallace Stegner

HIGH BORDER COUNTRY by Eric Thane

BLUE RIDGE COUNTRY by Jean Thomas

SHORT GRASS COUNTRY by Stanley Vestal

TOWN MEETING COUNTRY by Clarence M. Webster

FAR NORTH COUNTRY by Thames Williamson

In Preparation

BUCKEYE COUNTRY by Louis Bromfield

CORN COUNTRY by Homer Croy

BIG COUNTRY by Donald Day

RIP VAN WINKLE COUNTRY by Howard Fast

PINEY WOODS COUNTRY by John Faulkner

GREAT LAKES COUNTRY by Iola Fuller

PACIFIC NORTHWEST COUNTRY by Richard Neuberger

TIDEWATER COUNTRY by Elswyth Thane

GOLD RUSH COUNTRY by Charis Weston

MILE HIGH COUNTRY by Helen Worden

AMERICAN
FOLKWAYS

EDITED BY ERSKINE CALDWELL

LOWER PIEDMONT COUNTRY

by

H. C. NIXON

DUELL, SLOAN & PEARCE • NEW YORK

To

the Memory of

MY PARENTS

of

Piedmont, Alabama

R.F.D.

Contents

Acknowledgments

MANY PERSONS in various walks of life have furnished me
with bits of human material for this volume or have in other
ways facilitated my opportunity to see what is going on
among the people of the hill country. I am grateful to all,
though only a few can be mentioned here. Several have
found a logical place in my story, and others may recognize
themselves by circumstantial evidence. My characters are all
real, and any resemblance to fiction is purely coincidental.

The late Harry Dempsey, a local political leader of Piedmont, Alabama, took me with him on many trips which he
made for purposes of business, politics, or pleasure. We went
to barbecues, to other gatherings, and on fishing expeditions.

William N. Hay, assistant farm agent of Calhoun County,
Alabama, gave me the opportunity to travel with him over
the county and see farms and farmers in wartime.

Hughes Reynolds, of Rome, Georgia, gave me interesting
information about the Coosa Valley when he was writing his
book on that subject and when I visited him later.

Governor Ellis Arnall, his secretary, Melvin E. Thompson,
and Professor Cullen B. Gosnell of Emory University talked
with me about recent developments in Georgia.

Acknowledgments

I had visits and conversations with several newspaper men during the period of preparation. Among these were Austin Johnson of the Piedmont, Alabama, *Journal*, Barrett Shelton of the Decatur, Alabama, *Daily*, Harry M. Ayers of the Anniston, Alabama, *Star*, Roy Emmett of the Cedartown, Georgia, *Standard*, Tarleton Collier of the Louisville *Courier-Journal*, formerly of Atlanta, and Charles N. Feidelson of the Birmingham *News* and *Age-Herald*.

The "city fathers" of Guntersville, Alabama, gave me information about the transformation of that old farm-market center into a new tourist town on a TVA lake.

Members of the TVA staff deserve thanks for taking me on a delightful boat ride down the Tennessee River from Knoxville to Pickwick Dam, with four days for the trip and stops at towns, dams, parks, and other points of interest on the "Great Lakes of the South." This trip was for the purpose of pointing up a paper I was writing on *The Tennessee Valley: A Recreation Domain* in a Vanderbilt University social science series (1945), but it was also useful for the present work.

It should be mentioned that parts of this book show a kinship to certain magazine articles which I have written on related subjects, particularly "The New Deal and the South" in *The Virginia Quarterly Review*, Summer, 1943; "The South After the War" in the same magazine, Summer, 1944; and "Politics of the Hills" in *The Journal of Politics*, May, 1946.

Harnett Kane, author of *Deep Delta Country* and other works on Louisiana, suggested that I undertake the writing of a book on hill country folk and folkways. Professor Rich-

Acknowledgments

mond C. Beatty, of the English department of Vanderbilt University, read a few of the early chapters and rendered helpful criticism.

A summer grant from the Vanderbilt University Institute of Research and Training in the Social Sciences facilitated arrangements for me to get away from regular duties and make new journeys into the hill country.

The story, however, is my own, as is clearly indicated by the foreword. It is essentially an individual performance, and it even does not necessarily represent the views of my busy wife, Anne T. Nixon, who was so preoccupied with bringing in groceries and antiques that I had to stop writing at times to help her instead of having her assist me. In fact, she found no error of fact or form in the one chapter which she read. She was not critical.

This account is a one man's story about people for people, and it is offered rather consciously in the manner in which I used to cover rural personal items for a county newspaper, sometimes rounding out the space with biased comment.

H. C. N.

Nashville, Tennessee.

Foreword

MY CHIEF CREDENTIAL for writing this book is that I am a native, lover, and long-time resident of the country with which it is concerned. I am a product of the folkways of the hills. As I sometimes say, I was born in a house that burned, by the side of a dirt road that was changed, and across the road from a post office that was discontinued. This rural community, the subject of my *Possum Trot,* a volume which appeared in 1941, is between Atlanta and Birmingham and about a hundred and twenty miles from Chattanooga. It is in the Northeast Alabama county of Calhoun. When the century was young and I was a country correspondent for the *Daily Hot Blast* of near-by Anniston, I thus expressed my sentiment in newspaper verse:

THE WOODLAND HILLS OF OLD CALHOUN
> *I love their cool and pleasant shades*
> *Beside the sparkling streams,*
> *Where I may rest on soft green moss*
> *And soar in velvet dreams,*
> *Delighted with sweet melody*

That's pure and unrestrained and free.
Though I may travel far and wide,
Though I may sail the sea,
The woodland hills of old Calhoun
Will e'er be dear to me,
As dear as any place on earth,
And dearer as my place of birth.

My boyhood home was in a little valley, a tributary of the
Coosa Valley. It was about a mile northwest of the foot of
a small mountain range that was dominated by Chimney
Peak, which has an elevation of 1750 feet. This peak has always seemed to me to be a real mountain. It was youthful
pastime to climb Chimney, picking huckleberries in season,
sending large rocks crashing down the mountain side, and
observing the difference in time between seeing the steam
and hearing the sound from the locomotive whistle of a
train passing through the valley below. It was fun on autumn
nights to hunt 'possums in the woods between home and
mountain.

The sun rises over the mountain to light up my valley,
and the best rains come that way too. The ridge is beautiful
in springtime, when dogwood is in bloom and leaves are
green, alternating with patches of pine. The varied colors of
autumn and the occasional snows of winter make Chimney
impressive and unmonotonous. When careless hunters or
mischievous vandals set the woods on fire in dry weather in
autumn the flaming mountain at night gave me a feeling
that I was helplessly beholding a towering and terrible exam-

ple of super-personal power. It sometimes reminded me of the revival preacher's portrayal of hell.

Both of my grandfathers were Confederate veterans, one a slaveholder who came from upper South Carolina and the other a non-slaveholder from East Tennessee. They came from up-country to up-country when they settled in Alabama. My father was born at a Georgia hamlet then called Skin Chestnut. My mother was born not many miles from my native community. Irish blood was mingled with English and Scotch-Irish in my family tree, which in recent generations included such surnames as Green, Prater, and Davies.

I was one of eight children in a community where large families prevailed. As a boy I got my first idea of a high birth rate from an old Negro man. In conversation he answered my questions by mentioning that he had been married three times and was the father of twenty-three. By the first wife there were nine, by the second seven or eight, and by the third "only three." When I reminded him that those numbers did not add up to twenty-three, he set me right by merely saying, "There were two or three little fellows outside."

The fairly constant migration of families and individuals from Possum Trot early impressed me. Texas seemed a wonderful farm country. It attracted newly married couples, who sometimes wrote back to urge others to leave the "poor red hills" where they would never get ahead as hard-working farmers. Some of our people went to Oklahoma, or the Indian Territory. Others moved to Florida. Later there was migration to places like Birmingham, Detroit, Akron, Chicago, and various smaller centers, including cotton mill towns. Besides furnishing farmers and laborers, my community sent out into the world merchants, clerks, and teachers, along with a few preachers, politicians, and bootleggers. Few have come back to stay except for being buried or for getting back on the land because of unemployment in times of depression.

My first curiosity about race differences was caused by seeing a copy of a book, *The Negro a Beast,* which a few young white men were handing around and reading when colored fellows were not in sight. I could not harmonize that book with Alice Lee, a Negro tenant's wife who cooked delicious blackberry pies and let me sample them freely. It was clear to me that she could not be a beast. Then there was Charlie Dobbins, a colored farm worker who had a great collection of stories about Buffalo Bill, Frank and Jesse James, and Rube Burrow, a West Alabama outlaw. He could also give vivid accounts of such events as Bob Fitzsimmons' winning the heavyweight championship by knocking out Jim Corbett. He was too good a story-teller to be a beast.

In my young life, Jacksonville, four miles away, was "town," and Anniston, sixteen miles away was "city." I was at first less impressed by the city's stores and factories than by its policemen in uniform and its street cars which required neither horses nor locomotives to move along the main thoroughfares. My father gave me my first striking idea of economic change by telling me that he and his father once ground sorghum cane and made syrup on Anniston's Noble Street before it had street cars and a flow of commerce.

It might be said that I grew up behind the counter of a country store, and this experience shows up in many ways in

Foreword

these pages. Since my father was the storekeeper and also the postmaster for about forty years, I was at a good post for observing community growth and gossip. I there learned how much snuff and chewing tobacco it takes for a family to make a one-horse crop. I saw an abundance of horseshoe pitching in front of the store in summer time, and occasionally a crap game. I saw several fights and one shooting scrape. I saw three local men work a trick for arresting a bad fellow who was passing through, was carrying a Winchester rifle, and was wanted by the "law." One of the three admired the rifle and with seeming innocence got it in his hands, and then the other two appeared from nowhere, one with a drawn pistol and the other with a shotgun. They took their man under double guard to town to jail and collected a two-dollar fee. They enjoyed the experience of earning two dollars in that manner.

As a youngster I also worked in the field, plowing, hoeing, or picking cotton, especially at times of the day or week when trade was light at the store. Sometimes I had to cut sprouts or pile brush in a "newground," and Joe Badgett made a good partner for "newground" work. He could grab a medium-size snake by the tail, jerk it like a whip, and pop its head off.

There was one chore which I could never forget. A white sharecropper's wife had died, and the husband wanted to take her back by train to their former community. He had been on our place only for the year, and neighbors considered him "curious" and rather neglected him in the emergency. It became my duty to haul the unembalmed body more than a mile over a rough cotton field road to the station in a two-mule wagon, with the husband sitting on the seat beside me and others taking a short cut on foot to meet the train. It was late autumn, with signs of death on leaves and crops. I had read in the newspaper about the church trial of a Methodist preacher for views based on ideas of biological evolution. New science and old religion were battling in my mind, and did that sharecropper's wife have immortality after all? We exchanged few words, and my painful speculation took free play as the mules tramped slowly over the field. I looked at the coffin just behind me and doubted all that the country preachers had ever said, and then I worried keenly over the doubts.

When we were about two-thirds of the way we heard a passenger locomotive whistle blow. Our time seemed to be wrong, and we were about to miss the train. I lashed the mules, for I did not want the task of bringing the corpse back for another day. It might not be in condition for the train tomorrow. Maybe we could get in sight before it was too late and the train would wait. "Make it if you can," said the husband, and I lashed out at the mules again, prodding them into a good trot. The issues in my mind changed, and I now worried about a train, not the hereafter. The train came into sight and passed through without a stop. It was a freight train with a passenger whistle. I was relieved of worry in two ways. We made connection and the painful speculations were blown from my mind, partly for good.

The first school I attended was held in a church. Later we had a one-room school house, which was not ceiled. In cold weather we tried to keep warm by stuffing the stove with pine knots and coal and keeping it red-hot. We brought drinking water in a bucket from a spring at the foot of the hill, and sometimes at recess we tried to gang up and duck an out-of-school fellow who passed by and yelled "school butter."

I next attended the State Normal School at Jacksonville, going back and forth in the family buggy with other members of the family. Our dirt highway seemed to be always either dusty or muddy, and it was no easy task to make the eight o'clock classes in the morning. After college days at Auburn I came back to teach Alabama history and other subjects at this school, riding in daily from the country on horseback and working at store and farm on the side. Most of my pupils were from rural homes of North Alabama, some of them from tenant farms.

Times were good in our region in those years between 1910 and World War I. In spite of this fact or because of it, I went off to study at the University of Chicago, where I came under the teaching and influence of William E. Dodd, the American historian who was later to be Ambassador to Germany. From this native North Carolinian and from the readings required in his courses, I got my first appreciation of the difference and cleavage between the Southern Piedmont and the Southern lowlands, whether in Revolutionary times, the Civil War period, or after. I learned that Thomas Jefferson was a democratic product of the Piedmont, that his country and mine once constituted a part of the American West. This new learning was good for my soul. It changed my attitude toward the lowland plantation country, and I no longer had an occasional wish that my people might have been planters.

Foreword

The day before Christmas, 1919, I returned to Possum Trot from France, where my army service had been followed by a year of reference and research duty with President Wilson's Peace Commission at Paris. I was back from the center of the world community, with my head full of world problems. But my people were not interested in world problems or in hearing me talk about them. They were more interested in hog-killing weather, "forty-cent cotton," and the merits of different makes of tractors. Possum Trot cared as little about what was going on at Paris as Paris cared about what was going on at Possum Trot. The world community center and my neighborhood center did not recognize each other and they seemed to have little in common except an interest in Charlie Chaplin movies.

Somewhat disillusioned I took up teaching social science at Birmingham-Southern College on the Magic City's western border. There was more disillusionment as an intensive spell of hard times visited Birmingham and the whole cotton belt. This business slump was only a foreshadowing of the Hoover days in its measure of hard luck for Birmingham, but it seemed acute at the time. Burglaries and hold-ups brought on an informal curfew, with the police checking up on persons on the street at late hours at night. There was much begging, and prostitutes solicited trade from the porches and windows of shacks between the main railway station and the leading hotel. A group of our "prep" school boys, playing in swamp woods back of the college hill at recess, stumbled on twenty-five gallons of "prohibition" liquor concealed in milk cans under leaves. I heard rumblings of the Ku Klux Klan.

Foreword

It seemed to me that there was quite an interest in religion in Birmingham during this period of hard times. Baptist and Methodist services drew large congregrations. George R. Stuart, who had been associated with Sam Jones, "the mountain evangelist," was packing the First Methodist Church every Sunday with members and visitors. Henry M. Edmunds was making a popular appeal on a more modernistic basis at his Independent Presbyterian Church.

I taught in other Southern institutions, frequently passing through Birmingham to and from Possum Trot in days of the Coolidge boom, the Great Depression, and the New Deal. One year I spent several weeks in Atlanta and Birmingham as well as in other centers, conducting school forums on problems of the South under the general sponsorship of the United States Office of Education. The principal of a school under the shadow of a steel mill once adjourned the forum short of the time limit when a member of the audience offered a pointed comment and a pointed question about organized labor.

My father's death in 1928 provided additional important experience for me in the life of the hill country. As senior heir I was for several years the responsible agent in managing his estate, which included about two thousand acres in farm and woods and which for the period was undivided, unadministered, unencumbered, and unmarketable. I had to have good tenants and treat them like good tenants in order to hold things together, make ends meet, and avoid a depressed liquidation. I got a good response from whites and Negroes. Tenants and the estate generally broke even, showing more security than profit, and I can deny the charge that farm tenants as a class are worthless or shiftless or unreliable.

I became a critic of the Southern sharecropping system as a way of farming rather than of men as tenants or as landlords. I witnessed its decline in the hill country with little regret except missing the gathering and gossiping of sharecroppers at the country store or the central barn. Farm tractors tell no tales or jokes, and the mechanical cultivating machinery takes much of the human element out of farming as I have known it.

I always miss something when I go back to my old stamping ground in the hill country. I miss the church in the woods where I was "converted." It was disbanded years ago, and the deserted building burned. I miss the little school house under a big white-oak tree where I got a whipping. A school bus now passes by there to haul pupils four miles away to a consolidated school. I miss an old swimming hole, which has been ruined by a paved road and removal of the covering woods. I miss the four passenger trains and four freight trains that used to pass daily to or from Rome, Georgia. With buses, motor trucks, and other changes, it is enough to have one round-trip daily by a train combining freight and passenger service. I miss the late Luke Hudson, a colored sharecropper who served under four landlords in a period of fifty years without changing farms. Owners changed, but Luke never. He was buried in the farm graveyard. This book would be less if he had not crossed my path with his local lore.

I miss scenes and characters, but always "I want to go back, and I will." Back to Jacksonville and the neighboring

Alabama towns or settlements of Piedmont, Spring Garden, Bald Hornet, Possum Trot and Rabbittown. I hold with the workman who sang,

> *"If I live and don't get killed,*
> *I'm going back to Jacksonville."*

LOWER PIEDMONT COUNTRY

1

Annals of the Hills

"Goin' to Pigmount," said the unlettered farm workers when they took time off to visit the New South town of Piedmont, Alabama, around the turn of the century. They went to "Pigmount" for Saturday shopping, for industrial employment, and for celebrating the "Fo'th" of July. Occasionally a fellow would get to this town of the hills by "swinging" a freight train that was slowed down by a long and steep grade, such as the one at Bald Hornet four miles from town. Old-timers remember that before the days of modern equipment freight trains sometimes split in twain from broken couplings on this "Pigmount"-Bald Hornet stretch, and once a conductor in his stranded caboose was killed by a tail-end collision, with his engine section far ahead and his rear flagman, like himself, asleep from too many hours on duty.

It required some years for the rank and file to get on to the use and proper pronunciation of the name of Piedmont, which was chosen with geographical appropriateness and to be new. The former name was Cross Plains, ~~~~nstruction days the place had a Ku Klux Klan ~~~~~~ ~~ several Negroes and a Northern teacher of a Negro school. Partly to neutralize that stigma and to avoid offense to Northern capitalists, Cross Plains was banished from the map of the hill country, and Piedmont came into being, along with a land boom, a cotton mill, and the coming of a Yankee superintendent. The town shares its name with a college in North Georgia, an Atlanta hotel, a passenger train that hurries through the hills, a baseball league, and in other ways.

Piedmont exemplifies the physiography and the spirit of change of an upland border country of divides, gateways, and crossroads. It is near the center of a region which is marked out by the southernmost prongs and tongues of the Appalachian Mountains. This New South country now includes the larger cities of Birmingham, Chattanooga, and Atlanta, which is sometimes called the "gate city of the South." It contains such smaller cities as Bessemer, Gadsden, and Anniston in Alabama, and Rome on seven hills in Georgia.

This country is borderland between mountains and lowland plains, between mountaineers and cotton planters. It is land where the Appalachians, in their southwestward extension, fade away into small ridges and rolling hills. As the mountains disappear, the Piedmont Plateau on the east joins the Great Appalachian Valley, or series of valleys, on the west around the end of the Blue Ridge. In this end region the belts of long leaf and short leaf pines meet, with a mixture of various kinds of oak. At the eastern edge are sources

4

of streams that flow into the Atlantic, but the Coosa and the Chattahoochee Rivers flow to the Gulf, while the Tennessee drains the northwestern corner into the Ohio. The rainfall is over fifty inches a year, and erosion is severe in this area of red hills and cotton and roving "peckerwood" sawmills. Millions of tons of soil have moved to the sea since the Indians were removed from these hills slightly over a hundred years ago. "Gone with the Water" would be a more appropriate designation than "Gone with the Wind" for this region, which General Sherman passed through from Chattanooga to Atlanta and to the sea.

The major part of this land was the last from which the Indians were removed to homes west of the Mississippi. In it was the border between the Cherokees, who loved their upland fields, and the Creeks, who preferred land next to lowland streams. These Creeks and Cherokees were both "civilized tribes," as is emphasized by their descendants in Oklahoma today. Like other civilized peoples, they had border incidents and contests over land claims. At times they fought over hunting grounds and hunting practices. They were infiltrated by white traders and adventurers, and their squaws gave birth to mixed breeds. The town of Guntersville on the great bend of the Tennessee was founded by John Gunter, a Scotchman who had taken up life among the Cherokees.

Two great warriors crossed this hinterland of proud Indians and Indian towns, both of them with a destination that lay beyond and a purpose that meant no good to the red men. De Soto, on his winding route from Florida to the Mississippi, brought the first white men into the area. His expedition moved down the Coosa Valley, searching in vain for gold, and shifted to Mauvilla, or Tuscaloosa (later an Alabama town), where he had to fight a fierce battle that was virtually his undoing. Like Lee at Gettysburg, he moved away, reduced in strength and spirit. He left plenty of ill will behind him as he turned his course westward, destined to reach the Mississippi and be buried beneath its waters, where Indians could not disturb.

Two and three-quarter centuries later Andrew Jackson brought a band of Tennesseans across this up-country to punish the Creeks for a massacre in South Alabama, to break the power of their brave Red Eagle, and to open a great slice of Creek territory to land-hungry settlers and speculators from Tennessee and elsewhere. He was more successful than De Soto in fighting the Indians, and had better luck in opening up lands than the Spaniard had in finding gold. However, the Creeks retained an upper strip of their domain for two more decades.

The whites and Indians came into more conflict in the up-country when Jackson was President. Settlers and adventurers moved into Creek territory in North Alabama with little regard for Indian treaty rights, land surveys, or Federal authority. New counties in the area were laid out by the state. A white intruder was slain when United States officers undertook to take matters in hand. Civil war seemed to be in the air, with the Creeks in the middle, between the state and the nation. In the impasse President Jackson commissioned Francis Scott Key, author of "The Star Spangled Banner," to go to the Alabama capital and work out a settlement. Key performed his mission to the satisfaction of national and state administrations, whatever complaints the Creeks might have made, for the Indians were soon to go west. They could not stand in the way of a land boom.

Georgians in particular rushed into Cherokee areas in advance of treaty provisions, with a consequent issue between state's rights and Indian rights and a case of the Cherokee Nation *versus* Georgia before the United States Supreme Court. "Old Hickory" supported Georgia expansion and refused to do anything about the decision which Chief Justice Marshall rendered in favor of the Cherokees. He was quoted as saying, "John Marshall has rendered his decision. Let him enforce it." The discovery and mining of gold in the Dahlonega section stimulated the rush into the lands of the Indians. The Cherokees, like the Creeks, had to yield and go west on a "trail of tears" to the Oklahoma country. Many who refused to migrate were removed by force from their villages, homes, and fertile fields.

Among those who made the long march to the West in 1838 were Joe Vann and his wife, who left their brick house, which still stands on the road between the Georgia towns of Dalton and Chatsworth. Ralph McGill, of the Atlanta *Constitution,* visited the house in March, 1946, and gathered local lore about Vann, a violent man, with Cherokee blood in his veins. "He came," wrote McGill, "from somewhere in North Carolina, with the whisper following him that he was wanted for murder. He married a Cherokee woman and built the house of handmade brick, freighted by river boat and ox cart to the high hill. . . ." He sent his children to a near-by Moravian mission school. "He tried to make a go of it but the dice of destiny and the hunger of new settlers

7

for land and gold were too much for him. And too much for the Cherokees." The lands were sold by lottery, and with them the Vann house, which was then about half a century old. Here, says the story, John Howard Payne, author of "Home Sweet Home," was tried and acquitted after his arrest by the Georgia guard, who did not like his mingling with the Cherokees and his sympathies for the underdog.

New towns and counties came into existence in Northwest Georgia and Northeast Alabama, some of them named for Jackson and Jackson men. One county in each state bore the poetic name of Cherokee. In a few years only beautiful place-names were left to testify to Indian culture from Chicamauga to Sylacauga. Multitudinous streams significantly remain Indian waters. A roll call of those of the Coosa river system, for instance, is suggestive of rhythm and natural music. The Coosa is formed by the junction of the Etowah and the Oustanaula and, in turn, joins the Tallapoosa to form the Alabama. Between these junctions it is fed by such creeks as the Tallahatchee, Ohatchie, and Choccolocco.

These Indians had taken on many of the ways of the white man before their reluctant departure. A few, frequently of mixed blood, remained behind to become private landowners and even masters of slaves. An old Indian near Jacksonville, Alabama, expressed his ideas of racial rankings to Isaac Teague, a slave who knew a white father. The order of his classification was "white man, Indian, dog, and Negro."

Incoming farmers were soon staking out lands and settlements in the valleys vacated by the upper Creeks and the lower Cherokees. They generally avoided the mountains and semi-mountainous areas, parts of which were to remain in the ownership of the United States government, seemingly forever. To inhabitants of narrow valleys, however, the sharp ranges or mountainous hills could never be out of sight or out of mind. This mountain consciousness was reflected in the establishment of a Talladega, Alabama, newspaper, *Our Mountain Home.* All who have gone from this Piedmont country to prairie regions have ever missed the tree-covered hills and woodland springs.

The settlers came largely from Tennessee, the Carolinas, and older parts of Georgia, with smaller numbers from Virginia and other states. Covered wagons moved along valley roads which often had been Indian trails, and the site of an Indian village might become a white man's town. Early stage-line roads often approximated later rail routes. Many who came down the valleys did not stop but continued on to more spacious lands farther south or southwest. Gangs or droves of slaves came through on foot, sometimes moving and singing in unison. They did not know where they were going, but they were on their way.

Many of these settlers came from older upland regions, not from tidewater plantations. There were many families of Scotch-Irish stock from points farther up the Great Valley and from the Carolina foothills. There were members of plain Irish blood, including Georgia kinsmen of Dan Emmett, the author of "Dixie." A few descendants of French Huguenots moved in. However, people of English ancestry predominated.

In 1835 a group of families, "numbering forty or fifty souls," according to their chronicler. migrated in a body from Abbeville, South Carolina, to Cherokee County, Alabama. About the same time a group of Greens from the Greenville section of South Carolina acquired farm holdings fifty or sixty miles southwest of Rome. Hamilton Nixon, a native of Greenville, Tennessee, lived for a time not far from the Georgia town of Marthasville, which later became Atlanta, and finally settled on a small farm in Calhoun County, Alabama, with his large family. Melville Dwinnell, a native Vermonter, came south and established the Rome *Courier* in 1843.

These plain people of the hills, with few exceptions, were farmers rather than planters. Many of them were small farmers who were only slightly interested in growing cotton. They were primarily concerned with "livin' at home and eatin' in the kitchen." Some of them avoided cotton altogether as well as the tough red soil that produces it. They frequently sought the less fertile sandy soil, which was easy to cultivate or use for pasture. They handed this type of farming down to their children and their children's children, inspiring the Negro rhyme,

> *You can't raise cotton on sandy lan';*
> *I'd ruther be a nigger than a po' white man.*

Except in river-bottom communities, slaves constituted only ten to twenty-five per cent of the population, or less, in 1860. Most of the white families, including landowners, had no slaves. Many of the slave-owning farmers owned only a few slaves and worked in the field with them. Robert McCain came as a young man in 1845 from South Carolina to Merrellton, Alabama, to round out his ninety-four years as owner of six hundred acres and a couple of slave families, who remained with him after freedom. When he was getting ready for the first of his three wives, his prospective father-in-law came from a distance to look him over, arriving on a day not definitely scheduled. The older man found Robert McCain hard at work in the woods with his shirt off. Consent to the marriage was unqualified.

Most of these hill people were more interested in lands and farming than in books and learning. There were farm owners who could not read and write. Berry Moland was not unique when he touched the pen and made "his mark" to execute a deed to land in the Coosa Land District of Alabama, land which had been granted to the Molands by the United States over the name of President John Tyler. Backwoods speech was simple and generally to the point. Said one old patriarch, "I went to see my wife three times before we married. The first time I told her my business; the second time we set the day; the third time we had the wedding." A widower, making a first call with marriage in mind, came home and remarked that "Nancy gave me a cold potato." The plainness of speech, however, did not prevent the use of double words for emphasis, such as "widow woman," "boss man," "milk dairy," and "tooth dentist," which have been handed down, and I have heard a hill countryman effectively refer to a "dry drouth."

There were homes with enough books to fill a "secretary," including school books and very likely a "doctor book" on home treatment and herb remedies. More generally reading matter was limited to a "center table," on which the Bible might be prominent. A farmer who received and read a newspaper regularly and thoroughly was locally considered well informed. More conspicuous than books were shotguns and squirrel rifles, perhaps also a bottle or jug of liquor. Certainly there was more hunting than reading by many settlers in the Piedmont hills.

If the stay of Indians was long, the period of Negro slavery was short in the Piedmont hills, with the Civil War coming so soon after the opening of lands for settlement. The South's peculiar institution, though expanding, had not thoroughly spread over this region before the slaves were set free. The slave population, a minority by a wide margin, furnished much less than half the total labor. The status of these slaves, in many ways, was somewhat better than that of field hands in the regions of great plantations. That seems true, though the preserved facts of their life and work are more meager than the usual short and simple annals of the poor.

These observations on up-country slave life are mainly based on many scores of interviews with white and colored persons who lived in North Alabama during the days of slavery. I interviewed them thirty to thirty-two years ago and filled a little black filing box full of notes, which were supplemented by numerous letters in answer to a questionnaire. The first World War prevented my putting this material into a book, and I am just now getting around to using it. I got a favorable picture most generally from women who had been members of slave-owning families, while members of white families who did not own slaves cited some of the striking cases of cruelty. The Reverend Martin McCain, exslave, with whom I conversed for hours at different times, was eloquent on the good relations between slaves and members of the master's family. Crude and cruel features or instances were cited by "Aunt Julie" Carpenter, ex-slave and leading midwife of Tallahatchee Creek valley. Her oldest daughter was just thirteen years her junior.

Most of the up-country slaves worked on farms without the presence of a deputized overseer to drive them with tongue and lash. If the master or one of his sons was not with them, an able and trusted slave served as leader, perhaps by performing more labor than any other. Not a few slaves acquired rough or expert skills as carpenters, brick masons, blacksmiths, shoemakers, and the like. One of the best carpenters in my community prior to 1900 was Manuel Atkins, who learned his trade in slavery. Many slave women became seamstresses.

In rare instances skilled workmen accumulated savings and bought their freedom in an actual, non-legal sense. More commonly they hired their time from their masters by periodical payments and worked as free craftsmen. Such a case was Jim Rowland, who had money in his pocket and could read and write when he became a Rowland by purchase. He operated a shop at Jacksonville, Alabama, and invested all his Confederate money in leather when he foresaw that the South would lose the war, shrewdly declining to buy his freedom. Incidentally he gave his master's sons their first knowledge of Napoleon and Hannibal and the crossing of the Alps by those generals. He had a repertoire of stories similar to those of Uncle Remus.

Since inability to read and write was the rule, many craftsmen and leaders developed ingenious makeshifts. Some learned to read the printed figures on hand scales for weighing baskets of cotton in the field, remembered accurately the amounts brought in by the various pickers, and reported the amounts for each slave to the master. At times their correctness was confirmed by test through reweighing, in one specific case where there were seventy-five pickers, including children. Other leaders, with less power of memory, used original markings or symbols for names and amounts picked.

There were instances of slaves who acquired small sums of money by selling products grown or made in spare time, such as vegetables, gingerbread, and handicrafts. Most of the labor, however, was a matter of routine with little glamour or thought of profit.

Surplus slaves were sold off, sometimes, to distant points, or hired out by their masters. It was only by these practices that some masters could break even financially, and there were ways of encouraging the surplus, as by early marriages and by special privileges to mothers of large families. A woman who was promised her freedom if she would give birth to ten made it thirteen. There were unique as well as tragic aspects in selling slaves to be taken far away. It was said that Burl Williams was sold several times by his Coosa Valley master. Burl would return and be sold again, even if a former purchaser had to be repaid half the price for an unsatisfactory worker. A tricky master sold a good blacksmith, who had tuberculosis, in another state, before the disease could be discovered by the purchaser, and brought home the cash.

There were outlets for the expanding slave labor in the clearing and cultivating of "new grounds." Town occupa-

tions and beginnings of industrial activities attracted this
labor. Slave workers were tried out in small cotton mills, as
at Huntsville, Alabama, and around furnaces that burned
charcoal and made iron from red ore, which had been "dye-
rock" to the Indians and pioneers in the Birmingham region.
Slaves mined ore for the furnaces. Ethel Armes, in *The
Story of Coal and Iron in Alabama,* quotes the Anniston
story of a faithful slave miner, by the name of Vann, who
got a weekend pass to visit his wife but was killed on Saturday by a cave-in just before he was to leave. Slaves also
worked on construction jobs as railroad lines penetrated the
hills from lower river towns. Farmers in North Alabama, for
instance, moved with slaves and tents to work on the line
that was under construction from Selma toward Rome before 1860.

Hill farmers used various methods of providing food for
their slaves. Some reported the system of "allowance" of a
peck of meal and three and a half pounds of pork or side
meat a week to each active adult, with smaller portions to
children, and with slaves preparing food in their own quarters. One master said he killed a hog a year for every slave.
There were home-grown vegetables in season, and to the
monotonous diet wild meat was frequently added, for many
a slave family had a hunting dog. Flour from home-grown
wheat was occasionally offered instead of corn meal, and beef
sometimes was issued in place of pork. Syrup, or molasses,
might be added for Sunday. There were practices of old
slaves getting coffee by going to the mistress of the "big
house." Owners of only a few slaves might feed them in the
kitchen, with slaves and the master's family getting practi-

cally the same fare, though ham, sausage, and other special items were often reserved for the whites. A woman in Jefferson County, Alabama, fed a lone slave, a man, in a pan or bucket at the back door. A farmer near Piedmont put "potliquor" in a trough for slave children to eat in a merry scramble.

Slave quarters often consisted of substantial log cabins, with one or two rooms and a single fireplace for both heating and cooking purposes. The chimney was sometimes of brick but frequently a "stick-and dirt" construction. Furnishings and furniture were simple, if not crude, and there were instances of dirt floors. Sometimes the bedstead was provided by fastening boards to the walls in the corner of the room, with three corners of the bed thus supported and the fourth by a post. The bed was usually of straw, with rarer use of featherbeds. The cabins were not spacious for the number of occupants.

The coarse clothing for slaves varied between summer and winter, and there were instances of men wearing nothing in the field in warm weather but long-tail shirts. Such garments were more common for children. The clothing was made on the place, and at times the material.

Whipping was an important method of discipline. Where slaves were numerous, the curfew was enforced by community patrols. Unless a slave had a pass bearing his master's name, he had to dodge or outrun the patrol or take the consequences. So it was that

> *Nigger run, nigger flew,*
> *Nigger tore his shirt in two.*

The patrol at times got fun or excitement by chasing and catching slaves at night, particularly if young men were performing the function. Masters were sensitive about severe whippings by patrols, says a memoir, and "hard feelings were often engendered . . . especially if the patrolman's family owned no Negroes." Warren Harris, a Calhoun County farmer, once inflicted a torrent of profanity upon a patrol group for whipping slaves who had his written permit "to pass and repass" on the night they were whipped. A slave woman, caught at Jacksonville without a pass, made a Scriptural appeal to the Cross when two men took her, one by each arm, to administer the lash. She exclaimed, "Here I go, like my Master, between two thieves." The captors released their hold and hurried away from the sermon.

Long-period passes were frequently issued to a man who had a wife on another farm, the pass likely being good for weekends and for Wednesday nights. The husband had to be back on time for work on Thursday and Monday mornings.

The master's name was signed to many a pass without his knowledge by members of his family. Dr. J. D. Arnold, who spent his life at Jacksonville, said that when a boy he often forged passes for Marvin Scott, whom he considered "a good old slave."

The slaves for amusement and pastime had hunting, fishing, and dancing, with music from home-made instruments, singing, and tuneful calling of the turns. There were Christmas celebrations. Butler Green let his slaves go to a public hanging at Jacksonville. Corn shuckings were great occasions, which meant labor far into the night, with later eating and dancing, perhaps drinking. Saturday afternoon, once or twice a month, was time off from regular work, but this was not pure pastime, for there were personal duties, including washing clothes. "Aunt Julie" Carpenter knew slaves that got no holidays and had to do their washing on Sunday.

Slaves largely took to the religion of their masters, with Baptists and Methodists predominating in the up-country. There were a few of other denominations, including Episcopalian slaves of Episcopalian owners. Some of these, knowing no letter of the alphabet, could go through the entire Holy Divine Service. They enjoyed the responsive service, which Aunt Dinah explained as "talking back at the preacher." Slaves often worshiped in the same churches with the whites, using rear seats or a balcony and taking communion after the whites. There were exclusive Negro services in cabins and occasionally in other buildings, subject to white supervision or check-up lest subversive ideas be spread. Here the slaves could shout and sing their spirituals, with their own improvisings about "de golden stairs," "Jacob's ladder," "dem golden slippers," or "dat mornin' when de stars begin to fall."

There were fewer legally free Negroes in this up-country than in the older portions of the slave region. Laws had been enacted against freeing slaves within these states as well as against teaching them to read and write. But freedom could be inherited from a free mother, and there were thus cases of free Negroes in the hills. In my native community memory has handed down the names of "Free Charley," "Free Aitch," and the sisters "Free Mary" and "Free Martha." Their status was odd and insecure. They might have envied Hal Stypes, a slave neighbor, who learned to read, studied geography, and reached Canada by the "underground railroad."

The up-country contained white families who were as ill fed, ill clothed, and ill housed as the slaves, who had as little "edjication" as slaves, and more isolation. Some were landless, some were poor owners of poor lands, and some were "squatters" in rough corners "way back" in the hills where the soil would hardly sprout peas. Frederick L. Olmsted, a New York correspondent journeying in the Southern back country on horseback in 1853 and 1854, found nine North Alabama hill families dependent upon two oxen for all their hauling. There was no other transportation except on foot, often without shoes and over dim trails, not roads. Olmsted found a man, his wife, and children all working for a total wage of a dollar and a half a day. He saw half-naked women doing the rough work of men and white wage-hands working along with slaves. He found families living in filth in one-room cabins or shacks with no evidence of food for subsistence. There were wild berries in the spring and nuts in the autumn, hickory nuts, chestnuts, and chinkapins. There were acorns for razor-back hogs and grass for scrub cows and other livestock. Chickens were often seen scratching for food about the premises. Besides hunting game, some of the dwellers in the woods hunted "bee trees" and "robbed the bees" of wild honey. Many of these hillbillies had a lean and hungry look and a sallow complexion suggesting the term "clay-eaters," which slaves sometimes applied to them. More generally slaves and slave owners called them "po' whites" or "po' white trash."

Lowly poverty existed in many inaccessible portions of

the hill country, but it was less prevalent in this region than in the piney woods sections of the Southern lowlands. The upland valleys had a high proportion of non-slave-owning yeomen, who were more numerous in the antebellum South than has been generally supposed. They were not visited and described by Northern and foreign travelers as were the planters. The South's own romantic writers skipped them and gave too much attention to the brighter side of plantation society. So did a factual historian like U. B. Phillips, whose *Life and Labor in the Old South* is largely documented and flavored by plantation diaries, letters, and records. The critics of slavery also concerned themselves more with planters than with yeomen. Slaves, in turn, derided the "po' white trash" without making allowance for a middle class. But the important place of the small farmers and non-slave-owners in the antebellum South has been established from unpublished census returns and county records by Frank L. Owsley, Herbert Weaver, Blanche Henry Clark, and others of a new school of historians.

These sturdy farmers lived in houses that were less than elegant mansions but more than one-room huts. Olmsted, a critical observer, noted the neatness of some of these homes in North Alabama. Many of these farmers, through hard work by all members of the family, produced a comparative abundance for home consumption and something more for sale. In addition to grains, they raised livestock, including sheep and goats along with hogs, cattle, mules, and horses. They had vegetable gardens, and "sweet potato patches." Their poultry consisted of chickens, geese, guineas, and turkeys. They got honey from their own "bee gums," which might be sections sawed from hollow trunks of gum trees, with cross sticks to hold the honey and covering over the tops. They grew apples and had apple cider. They turned their farm products into such items as clothing, shoes, baskets, brooms, soap, beeswax, persimmon beer, and maybe, liquor.

The men of the hills varied as widely as the lands, and there were gradations, not sharp divisions, between the best farmers and the ne'er-do-wells. Many improved their living conditions between 1850 and 1860, while others became "whipped down" and gave up. There were opportunities for moving up, with frontier lands still available.

White laborers found other work besides farming. There were sawmills in the hills before the Cherokees departed, with logging and hauling requiring men and teams. White men as well as slaves worked in iron ore mines, and white men were active in operating various little furnaces and foundries, which were destroyed by Yankee raiding forces during the Civil War but nevertheless foreshadowed the shape of greater things to come. The furnaces consumed not only iron ore, but also limestone for fluxing and acres upon acres of trees in the form of charcoal. Beginnings were made in the use of stone coal.

The chronicles of one of these outmoded and deserted villages emphasize the role of water power. The village was Polkville near the present site of Anniston, on Cane Creek, a few miles from where that stream enters the Coosa River. A creek dam furnished water to run a furnace, a forge hammer, a machine shop, a grist mill, and a sawmill. The equipment for the air blast was a wooden box of about three thousand cubic feet and twenty feet high. Water from the dam poured in at the top and created a whirling current at the bottom, with air escaping through a pipe from the box to the furnace. The forge hammer, weighing six hundred pounds, was lifted by a water wheel with cogs and dropped on an anvil for beating out wrought iron. Its boom, boom, boom could be heard for miles beyond the creek.

A dozen white families furnished labor at these iron works, with slaves performing much of the common labor. The village had a commissary, a general store, and a doctor. It stimulated activity up and down Cane Creek.

This antebellum village sent products to Rome and in greater amounts down the Coosa to such points as Wetumpka, Montgomery, Selma, and Mobile. Flatboats were made on an adjacent creek. Only the upper third of the Coosa was navigable upstream, and boating from the village to Wetumpka was extremely hazardous and possible only with a good flow of water. There were numerous shoals and rapids, including the "devil's staircase," to plague the boatman until twentieth-century improvements came along.

As the Coosa rushed over the steps of the "staircase," dashed against metamorphic reefs, and poured into whirling pools, it created a roar that was heard for miles. Here was the final leap from uplands to lowlands, and here was the final test of the boatman's skill as he guided his load of iron or lumber or cotton into steamboat waters. Just below lay the entrepot of Wetumpka, at the Coosa-Tallapoosa junction, where dealers and agents were ready to take over rafts and freight from the up-countrymen for shipment down the Alabama. The up-countrymen made their return overland, and often had to become footmen as they hit the trail homeward. They have handed down stories of covering as much as ninety miles in two days.

Only the lower third of the Chattahoochee permitted regular navigation, for, as that river wound through the Georgia hills, it had to "run the rapid and leap the fall." The Tennessee had its Muscle Shoals, which could be navigated only when the water was high.

As the hill country developed, transportation and transportation problems became important in this region. Ways were sought to avoid fifty or a hundred miles of wagon hauling to reach the markets of Atlanta, Rome, Chattanooga, Nashville, and Wetumpka. Steamboating began on the upper Coosa system in 1845, furnishing traffic between Rome and the Alabama village of Greensport. There was earlier and greater steamboat transportation on the Tennessee. Promoters sought to unite the Coosa and Tennessee systems by canal and even to reach the Atlantic by linking the Ocmulgee with the Coosa. The schemes came to nought.

Railroads were planned to supplement or feed river traffic. Atlanta got the first of its three names, Terminus, in 1837, as the end of a proposed state railroad. Lines were stabbing at the Tennessee Valley, both as east-west and north-south routes. Planters along the Alabama wanted to reach Atlanta as well as to tap the Coosa and Tennessee River regions by rail. Their Alabama and Tennessee road was constructed from Selma through Talladega and by 1861 it had reached Blue Mountain, just beyond the present site of Anniston. But the coming of war suspended its construction and that of other lines in the hill country.

Lower Piedmont Country

The Civil War found the newly settled up-country pretty much isolated in its stage of development and in its general outlook. It still had much more land in virgin timber than in cultivated crops. It hardly had an urban center large enough to be called a city. Atlanta was young and, in reality, only a town. Many cities and towns had not yet become names on the map. The region was playing only a subordinate role in the politics of the three states in which it lay. But, as strategic crossroads country, it was to see raids and counter-raids. It was to discover itself and be discovered.

2

Civil War and After

=====

WHEN the Civil War came the hill country did not have enough slaves or cotton or planter railroads to give it the outlook of the lowlands. It was quite different from the country below the falls of the rivers. Many of its people wished to be left alone and to have no truck either with slaves and slaveowners or with the politics of "Abe Linkhorn."

The hill people were not ardent for secession. There was talk of forming a pro-Union state in North Alabama, perhaps including adjacent counties of Georgia and East Tennessee. Jefferson County, in which Elyton was to become Birmingham, and all Alabama counties to the north, except one, chose "cooperationists," not "secessionists," to the state convention that adopted secession. The exception was a proslavery county, with several planters from South Carolina, which had recently changed its name from Benton to Calhoun to honor a Southern state's-rights champion instead of a moderate Missourian.

The prevailing opinion in the hills favored watchful waiting rather than precipitate action. Many North Alabama leaders were looking to the state of Tennessee, which was slow to consider secession. Some even spoke of secession from Alabama and annexation to Tennessee. The hill delegates insisted in vain upon a popular vote on the secession issue. When W. L. Yancey, the state's leading secessionist, intimated that the obstructing "cooperationists" were traitors, Nick Davis, of Madison County in the Tennessee Valley, challenged him to come with his force and warned that "we will meet him at the foot of our mountains, and there, with his own selected weapons, hand to hand, face to face, settle the question of the sovereignty of the people." The Davis men, strongly and overwhelmingly supported in the hills, were outnumbered and outvoted in the convention.

Thus the hill people took up arms but at times complained that the contest was "a rich man's war and a poor man's fight." Many of them denounced the exemption from Confederate conscription of planters owning twenty or more slaves until the "twenty-nigger law," as they called it, was repealed. It was not strange that secret peace societies eventually developed in the hills, with sympathy for numerous Southern deserters. Nor was it strange that the Union recruited several companies and found other forms of aid in this region.

Once the decision for war was made, most of the leaders of the hills took up the cause of the Confederacy, though they could not carry all their followers with them. Many tough fighters came out of the hills to battle for the Southern cause in campaigns from the Potomac to the Gulf. And Georgia's northwest corner county of Dade, which saw the bloody battle of Chicamauga, did not haul down the Confederate flag from its courthouse until July 4, 1945.

The people of the up-country knew the last half of the Civil War at close range, with many civilians becoming acquainted with the warning, "The Yankees are coming." They had the experience of hiding valuables and rushing livestock to backwoods away from roads. They had the experience of seeing the Yankees ride up before such precautions could be taken. On one occasion when Yankee soldiers were taking mules and horses from the barn of a Green family near the Georgia-Alabama border, Grandma Green armed herself with a butcher knife from the kitchen, stood at the door of the stable of her saddle horse, explained that the horse was for her own private use, and said she would stick that knife in the first soldier to touch her horse. They let woman and horse alone, the officer in charge observing to his men that "a woman with that much nerve is entitled to a saddle horse."

These people were close to the campaigns around Chattanooga, the Sherman movement from Chattanooga to Atlanta, and the fall of Atlanta. These actions, which cut across the Confederacy and doomed it, were supplemented by raids farther south in the hill country by Union forces under Generals Wilson, Rousseau, and others, with the destruction of various iron works which had been making supplies for the Southern army and navy.

The hill country has its own collection of stories and memories of Civil War times. It acquired a strong respect for General Sherman, whom Henry Grady described in New York as an able man, "kind of careless . . . about fire." Hill people long recalled Joseph E. Johnston's retreating strategy that limited Sherman's activities and delayed his army for days and weeks in North Georgia in 1864. They criticized the removal of Johnston, an up-country favorite, as the fighting reached Atlanta. There were Confederate veterans who never ceased talking about "Fightin' Joe" Wheeler, the hundred-pound man "who wasn't afraid of nothin' and nobody." This Georgia general, who later lived in North Alabama and fought in the Spanish-American war, was widely quoted in country stores when newspapers reported him as calling on his men at the land battle of Santiago to "give the Yankees hell," meaning the Spaniards.

Bedford Forrest was the hero of the most dramatic exploit that occurred in the Lower Piedmont Country during the Civil War, an exploit marked by his statue on Rome's Broad Street at the head of the Coosa. This Cossack of the Confederacy was without formal schooling, military training, or aristocratic background, but had won success before the war as a Mississippi planter, slave trader, and Memphis business man. A natural leader, he moved up as brilliantly in military activities as in private affairs. It has been said that he was "born a soldier as other men are born poets." Profanity was his poetry.

There were elements of comedy and hardship, with a Paul Revere feature, in the running fight across North Alabama in 1863 between Forrest's cavalry and Colonel Abel D. Streight's Union infantrymen, who were mounted on mules. Streight left Nashville in the spring, with men and mules loaded in boats, and, after moving down the Cumberland and up the Tennessee, he struck out by land from Eastport,

Mississippi. His purpose was to sweep behind the Chattanooga forces of the Confederacy, destroy the arsenals at Rome and Dalton, and cut the railway supply line between Atlanta and Chattanooga. To Forrest fell the task of following him, detecting his purpose, and checking him.

Streight's rear guard fought back effectively as the two forces moved from the Tennessee Valley over Sand Mountain to Gadsden. But the Yankees had mule troubles. The animals exposed their whereabouts by braying, and many gave out because of distemper, or "train cold," contracted on the boat. A few hundred were scattered and lost by a stampede caused by enemy scheming. However, Streight was able to get fresh mules along the way, and he reached Gadsden with his force intact. Then began the race up the Coosa Valley for Rome, about seventy miles away by the roads of that time.

Streight sent two hundred men in a hurry to hold the river bridge at Rome, which was undefended, being seemingly safe behind the zone of battle. He followed with the other fifteen hundred and sought to give attention to Forrest, who was temporarily checked at the Black Creek bridge, which Streight crossed and burned.

Two civilians here entered the picture and changed the outcome of events. Emma Sansom, a country girl, showed Forrest a forgotten ford, riding behind him part of the way and walking with him part of the way to the place and getting a Yankee bullet through her dress. Taking a lock of her hair, the general left the girl, and his cavalry was soon across the creek, closer upon the heels of the "mule brigade" than the enemy dreamed.

The other civilian was John Wisdom, ex-stage-driver and former resident of Rome, who was then living at Gadsden. Trying to return to Gadsden from a visit east of the river, he found his ferryboat wrecked and learned that Union soldiers had passed through Gadsden and on up the west bank of the Coosa. Without knowing about Forrest, who later sent a messenger ahead, Wisdom got a horse and "lit out" up the east bank for Rome. The horse fell exhausted after going twenty-two miles. He exhausted four other horses and a mule en route, and walked a spell before getting the last horse on which he rode into Rome at midnight.

Old men and boys of Rome, with help from farmers called in, assembled at the bridge with squirrel rifles, shotguns, and two antiquated cannon. They had oil-soaked hay ready to fire the wooden structure if they could not hold it. If all reports are true, they also had a supply of whiskey at the bridge. When the men of Streight's flying column appeared and looked over the situation from a hill, they decided not to fight and turned back to rejoin their main body.

In the meantime Forrest had overtaken and surprised Streight in the woods near Lawrence, Alabama. The Yankees had wasted time and energy the preceding night through road confusion at a spot where wood-haulers had made tracks in all directions. It was nine in the morning, and they had stopped to rest and feed the mules. Streight said that "nature was exhausted," for his men fell asleep in battle line under fire from the Rebels, who half surrounded them and suddenly stirred up a noise that suggested a much larger force, moving their two guns about a hill in the distance as though several batteries were coming up. Forrest demanded surrender. Streight yielded, stacked arms, and marched his men down into a hollow before realizing that he was surrendering over fourteen hundred men to fewer than five hundred. Then "he did rear," reported Forrest who just laughed at him. Prisoners and captors, mules and horses, moved on to Rome, meeting Streight's returning two hundred, who also became prisoners and got to Rome after all. Death soon claimed nearly half of the fine horses that brought the hard-riding Rebels from Tennessee to Rome. It was the end of a rough journey for them.

The Romans had a holiday, with food for the hungry and liquor for the thirsty. Streight was offered drink, but he was in no mood for festivities, and Forrest departed for Tennessee without waiting for the town to celebrate its good luck. Rome was to give John Wisdom four hundred dollars and a silver service, besides compensating a widow for furnishing him one of the horses which he exhausted. The Alabama legislature awarded Emma Sansom a section of public land for her performance in showing Forrest where to ford Black Creek, and in time Gadsden erected a monument to her.

The pursuit, bluffing, and capture of Streight would alone be enough to call forth the military epigram about getting there "fustest with the mostest," which has been erroneously but appropriately attributed to Forrest's coinage. A little group of Rome citizens have organized to deny and disprove that Forrest ever used those words and to point out that he said, "I took a short cut and got there first." It is clearly true that "fustest" and "mostest" are not in the colloquialism of the region. But Forrest would have been true to the idiom of the hills in saying, "Git thar fust with the most." That expression would fit Forrest.

The hill country, had a heavy dose of hard times when the tide of war changed and surrender came. It had aided both sides and had lost movable property to both sides. It had been crossed by Union and Confederate forces. Its means of transportation, whether rail, boat or beast of burden, were reduced or disrupted. There was little to sell and scarcely a market to sell in. Growing food on the farm and eating it furnished one hope of life. But that required time, and it was said that good seed had run out in the period of the Confederacy. Crops were pretty poor in 1865 and 1866. Wild animals, which had increased in wartime, were hunted and eaten as never before. There were cases of starvation, and widows died seeking food for their children. There were examples of families living in the woods with only tree tops and branches for shelter. Destitution among the whites was far greater in the uplands than in the lowlands. Thousands of whites in the hills got relief rations from the Freedman's Bureau and other sources. Thirty-five thousand persons, white and colored, in the counties around Atlanta were dependent upon public aid during the first winter after "surrender." In March, 1866, the Georgia legislature appropriated $200,000 to buy corn for the poor. By 1868 there was a let-up in privation and public relief. Crops were better, and railroad construction was underway. Merchandise was coming in from the East and Middle West.

There were many up-country Republicans after the war. Some of these were prominent leaders, though the label "scalawag" was placed on native whites who were willing to cooperate politically with the incoming Republicans, or "carpetbaggers," and with the newly enfranchised Negroes. The hill country also contained a large number of Democrats. Republican groups and planter Democrats competed for the support of the white voters of the hills and for the control of the postwar railroad development, which offered great opportunities for financial manipulation, especially through state sponsorships and bond endorsements. The Democrats had the first legislative inning, before the freedmen got the suffrage, and started state governments off in the game of railroad financing. They also undertook to control Negro labor through the enactment of special "black codes." Then Congress and the army took charge, denying the vote to Southern planters and colonels and extending the suffrage in general to the Negroes, who gave the Republicans a big inning. Finally, the Democrats came back at the end of Reconstruction and reduced the Negro's political power.

Race issues and railroad ventures were in politics, and the hill people were divided on them. There were contests, conspiracies, and physical brawls between rival finance-politicians, some playing up the issue of "white supremacy," others going along with "black Republicans." Interests and leaders back of lines from Cincinnati to Chattanooga and into Alabama at one stage might have been called a "black team." Several Democratic leaders who were financially and officially connected with lines which became the Louisville and Nashville system were distinctly a "white team," with important support from the city of Louisville.

L. and N. Democrats and Conservatives were among those

who espoused the cause of "white supremacy," home rule, and home capital. They fought the railroad interests represented by such Yankees as Jay Cooke of Philadelphia, Russell Sage of New York, and the Stantons of Boston. Through the Louisville press they hurled charges against Cincinnati for that city's political and financial invasion of the hill country, especially its extending rail connection to Chattanooga. They called to the hills to deliver the plantation country from "black Republicans." One of their members was George Houston, the "Bald Eagle of the Mountains" of North Alabama. This anti-Calhoun Conservative and former railroad director was elected governor of Alabama in 1874 as the white hope to end the era of Reconstruction and undo the state railroad financing of the Republican regime. He performed his task well. Planters and local industrialists, including L. and N. interests, wrote a new state constitution with rigid state and local tax limits. But the L. and N. had been hit hard by the panic of 1873 and came under Eastern and foreign ownership. Southern white supremacy and Northern financial supremacy came together in terms of peace and harmony.

Other things were happening while the railroad scramble was going on. Many men of the hills joined the Ku Klux Klan, which through chance was started by a group of pranksters at Pulaski, Tennessee, in 1866, was later organized on a Southwide basis at Nashville, and came under the leadership of General Forrest as its Grand Wizard. Bedford Forrest, who took up insurance business and headed a disastrous railroad venture, was no stranger to the hill country, which he visited again on business and on missions for the Klan.

This organization, by secret methods and hooded pageantry, sought to check the concerted activities and political practices of carpetbaggers, scalawags, and Negroes. It opposed the Union League, or Loyal League, which operated in the South as an agency for aiding freedmen, the Republican Party, and Northern investors. The K.K.K. was officially limited in membership to Confederate veterans. In the spirit of feudalistic knighthood, it defended and protected Southern womanhood. It stood for law and order on the basis of white supremacy. "White man—right or wrong—still the white man." That was the masthead motto of a Tuscaloosa, Alabama, newspaper, which was edited by a Klansman.

The Klan of 1867 and 1868 often influenced the conduct of Negroes by methods that were short of physical force or violence. Peter Hunt, ex-slave and later a landowner in my rural section, once had a contact with the "Ku Klux," which illustrated this technique. He answered a call at his front door late one night, and horsemen robed and masked, demanded a drink of water. When he started to hand one a dipper of water, the man insisted that he bring the bucket, which the rider presumably emptied down his throat without stopping (with the use of a concealed rubber bag). He handed the bucket back to Peter with the comment, "That's my first drink of water since I was killed at the battle of Shiloh." The interview and words of advice came to an end with one of the visitors saying, "Let's go; we've got to be in Montgomery in ten minutes." The riders dashed away, and the visit keenly impressed Peter Hunt, who knew that Montgomery was more than a hundred miles away.

The robed riders roamed the hills, frequently dominating

local government and determining local elections. They issued mysterious warnings, and they sometimes took desperate measures if warnings were not heeded. Fighting and lynching were carried on by Klansmen, collectively or individually, or by others acting under the name and cover of the organization. After about two years of wide activity, the organization was abandoned and disbanded by the top leaders, with the observation that its purpose had been attained. Many of the later abuses were disowned by bona-fide members of the Klan. Volumes of testimony about it were collected by an investigating committee of Congress, three from Alabama alone. Forrest and other generals made baffling witnesses. Local courts were also baffled. I knew of a fellow who said he escaped conviction because he was a "damn good Klansman."

The Klan and the Klan issues left a stamp on the hillside. The contest which this organization waged had a long-range effect on the mind, outlook, and political ways of the hill people. To a degree it restored the spirit and pattern of the antebellum patrol in race relations. The patrol dealt with the slave; the Klan with the slave become free. Fearful of civil strife and race equality, many yeomen whites joined the robed riders in order to "put the nigger in his place." For reasons of their own, they supported the planters in opposing and overthrowing the political coalition of white Republicans and Negroes to bring an end to the "dark days of Reconstruction" and restore "home rule" in the Southern states. They got "home rule." At the same time they got less corruption in government and less support for public schools. The home-rulers limited taxes to invite new capital.

With true consistency, the men of the hills were later to oppose the lowland planters and the planter-controlled Negro voters in the agrarian crusade which culminated in the Populist movement. They were ready for the revival of the Klan in a new form after the first World War. If some of them, on Sand Mountain and elsewhere, remained or became Republicans, they were likely to insist on being "lily-white Republicans." If they joined labor unions, they wanted Negroes to stay out or perhaps be segregated in separate units, at least until the CIO came along with a policy of solidarity. They looked upon the Farmers' Union at first as a white man's union.

The white inhabitants of many little communities and villages in the hills kept Negroes away for periods extending into the twentieth century. If a Negro came through one of these places, he must not let the sun go down on him there. In this era the communities that had Negroes and Negro workers wanted them, while those that had them not wanted them not. But the communities of both types were alike in accepting the white man's emphasis on white supremacy and in a responsiveness to the politician's appeal to that emphasis, even for using it as a smoke screen for serving vested interests. This indoctrinated folkway meant that the Negro must never again have the power which he had when the Ku Klux Klan first rode forth to check him. Never again must the colored man be able to say to the white man, "The bottom rail's on top now, Mister."

The hill country, in spite of its immediate hardships, lost less in general than the lowlands from the effects of the Civil War and Reconstruction. It experienced less upheaval in its way of life and work. It had less private wealth tied up in slaves, plantations, and plantation mansions. It had less to be destroyed, either of wordly goods or of the grand manner of living. It emerged with less isolation and more opportunity to grow cash crops and market them. Its mineral resources and other resources became known to members of the Union and Confederate armies who passed though its valleys during the war. Before the turmoil of Reconstruction was over, Northerners, coming south, and lowland Southerners, coming north, were meeting and mingling in the hill country for the purposes of railroad building, industrial development, and business speculation, including real-estate booms. These leaders, as one traveler observed, were to make this country a land of "Southern Yankees." Many traditions, outside the body of racial attitudes, were soon to pass away under the spell of a "New South" gospel, a gospel which grew up lustily in the hill country. The chief preacher of that gospel was Henry Grady, a native of North Georgia, who started a newspaper career in the hill town of Rome.

3

Worship of Industry and Business

WHAT was to be the name of the new newspaper projected for the new town of Anniston, which had hopes of becoming an industrial metropolis in the mineral belt of Alabama? That was the topic of conversation among a group of men on the porch of the town's chief inn one day in the middle eighties. Henry Grady, visiting editor from Atlanta, was in the party. From the inn on a hill the glare of an iron furnace was visible, and this gave an inspiration to Grady, who said, "Why not call it the *Hot Blast?*" Thus Anniston had a *Daily Hot Blast* until a newspaper merger ended its identity twenty-five years later. This paper symbolized the industrial mindedness of the Lower Piedmont Country, the New South's Ruhr region where heavy industries and abundant labor were coming together.

The hill country had led the low country in passing out of the era of defeat and despair, thanks to the opening of mines, the establishment of furnaces and mills, the spread of lumbering, and the construction of railroads, along with a restored and expanded cotton crop. The military invasion was over. The political carpetbag invasion was over. The widely relished invasion of capital and capitalists was now the order of the day.

Town-making and city-building had supplanted war-making and the "radical" politics of Reconstruction. Atlanta had recovered from the ravages of war and become the capital of Georgia, to the loss of the midland town of Milledgeville. This city had made strides amid the graft and extravagance of the carpetbag regime, when H. I. Kimball manipulated state funds for deals in railroads and real estate, including a hotel and an opera house, which was turned into a state house, and his acquisitive political power called forth the colored legislator's tune,

> *H. I. Kimball's on de flo',*
> *'Tain't gwine ter rain no mo'.*

The Atlanta railroads were burdened with traffic, and Robert Somers, a Scotch visitor, writing a few years after the Civil War, found Northern capital and "a class of aspiring Northern men" the chief reason for the city's progress.

Extensive iron developments around Chattanooga were carried on by a Northern general, who had fought in the region, and who had associates as well as capital from Ohio and Indiana. Through the influence of Ohio investors, an Alabama iron town between Chattanooga and Atlanta was shrewdly named Tecumseh, not for the Indian chief, but for William Tecumseh Sherman. Sam Noble, an Englishman who had made Confederate cannon at Rome, founded the postwar town of Anniston, partly with Yankee money. Philadelphia capital came to Cedartown, Georgia. Daniel Pratt, South Alabama pioneer industrialist, moved, with his son-in-law, Henry F. DeBardeleben, into the Birmingham area, where, as George Leighton says, "one after another Northern iron men arrived to join the group of Southern speculators." They organized towns and companies and also built furnaces. The day in 1873 when the Pratt-De Bardeleben furnaces went into blast dogs started up a deer and "ran him full speed clean over the pig bed." In a few years the seemingly ancient history of the "Pittsburgh of the South" was compressed in the jingle,

> *In eighteen hundred seventy-one,*
> *When Birmingham was Elyton.*

The areas of Birmingham and Chattanooga came to be linked industrially through the Tennessee Coal, Iron and Railroad Company, or T. C. I., which was chartered first in Tennessee, then finally in Alabama, where its major interests developed. In the meantime T. C. I. had become a Wall Street issue in the panic of 1907 and was taken in as a subsidiary by the United States Steel Corporation, with the financial house of Morgan playing a powerful role in the negotiations. Thus coal and the Indian's red "dye-rock" of the hills came to be annexed to a multi-billion-dollar industrial empire.

The heavy industries of the up-country had to have better transportation facilities than could be provided by precarious river traffic and short-line feeder railroads. Immediately after the Civil War, the rail lines of the hills were restored and extended, first with state bonds and heavy takings by political promoters, and then with funds from private investors in the East and abroad. In short order, the three cities of Atlanta, Birmingham, and Chattanooga were connected by trunk lines that formed a major triangle and gave the new industries an outlet to all corners of America. The triangle became links in the Southern Railway system, organized under J. P. Morgan sponsorship to "serve the South" from Washington, D.C., to New Orleans. Into this system by lease came the road from Cincinnati to Chattanooga, which the city of Cincinnati constructed in 1869 to tap Southern resources and expand the use of Cincinnati products, such as buggies, clothing, and even architecture.

Human sidelights on the development of the network that became the Southern system were exemplified in the personal career of John Thomas, whose service on the rail linked two eras and two regions. As a young locomotive engineer in Civil War days, he hauled freight for the Confederacy in the Selma area of Alabama, finally fleeing southward in his engine, with his wife and children in the caboose. He declined opportunity to take personal possession of a shipment of cotton, for it seemed too much like stealing. So the Yankees got it. As a patriarchal engineer in the first part of the twentieth century John Thomas was running a passenger train between Meridian, Mississippi, and Rome, Georgia. Sitting erect at the throttle, he hustled from plains to hills and back again, crossing the whole state of Alabama daily for years, with an individual whistle rhythm that every plowboy knew or thought he knew. Workmen gauged the time of day by the sound of his whistle, often singing out, "Ol' John Thomas, he can't be late!" If he got behind time, he made it up. If his train and one on a parallel line came along at the same time, John Thomas left the rival behind. He mixed new ways and old ways by becoming an active member of the engineers' brotherhood but refusing to participate in national convention affairs on Sunday. He dedicated his *Fifty Years on the Rail* to his union brothers, urging them to read the book but not to lend it, for he wanted sales.

More significant than the Southern for the Birmingham district was the construction or consolidation of lines that constitute the Louisville and Nashville Railroad. This company entered the district dramatically in 1871-72, taking over the incomplete South and North line between Birmingham and Decatur, which had been aided by Alabama state bonds. This hooked up with lines above Decatur and fulfilled the iron men's cry of "on to Nashville." It prevented Russell Sage interests from blocking things and annexing Birmingham industrially to Chattanooga. It was to give Alabama mineral products additional outlets to Northern cities and to the Gulf. The crucial deal was consummated at Louisville, where negotiators came to physical blows in the Blue Parlor of the Galt House, with Kentucky whiskey being served successfully to restore fellowship and turn the group from deadlock to decision.

The L. and N. in the next decade completed a belt line around the Birmingham district. This "Alabama Mineral" division, a two-hundred-mile race track except for lack of speed, linked up such points as Anniston, Gadsden, Ensley, Calera, Sylacauga, and Talladega, with a dozen offshoots to mining towns and with the main line cutting across the division like an arrow. Birmingham and the L. and N. owe a heavy debt of development to each other.

It was the hard-headed vision of railroader Milton Hannibal Smith that tied the L. and N. so intimately with the Birmingham district. Through the ladder of promotion, starting as freight agent, he became head of the L. and N. in 1882 for a life tenure of twenty-eight years. A native of rural New York, he had removed to Mississippi and served as a railroad yardmaster or dispatcher at Chattanooga and elsewhere during the Civil War. It is said of him that he handled trains, as a good economic man, first for the Confederate army, then for the Union forces. His first acquaintance with Alabama was through a short period of work on the road that long knew the services of John Thomas.

Smith's formula for progress made a strong appeal to the coal barons and steel magnates of his day. He was a hog for freight, especially for long-haul freight. But he despised passenger traffic because one could "not get a g—— damn cent out of it." He hated Jim Crow segregation for its increased cost. He showed little interest in decent passenger stations or joint terminals, whether at Birmingham, Atlanta, or other cities. For a ticket to the promised land, a hill-country preacher urged his flock to avoid the "Hell 'n N."

If the L. and N. wanted all that the traffic would bear, Smith knew how to put freight rates low enough to save traffic and make traffic. He hauled Alabama coal to New Orleans on terms that put it in competition with river-borne coal from the Ohio country. He was ever ready to give rail connections and run spur tracks to new mines and

44

furnaces. Produce the freight, he urged them, and he would haul it, on his back if necessary.

He fought labor unions and handled strikes without mercy. His was a policy of low wages, and, with genuine consistency, he opposed increases in his own salary. Public regulation of railroads and other utilities was foreign to his philosophy. As an anti-reformer, he was a power in every state capital from the Ohio to the Gulf, with plenty of legal and political henchmen to do his bidding. Yielding hard to the new controls, he made the complaint, "Too many people have the vote." He was severely criticized and abundantly praised. "One and all, to a man, the coal and iron men of Alabama stand up for their chief," wrote Ethel Armes of him in her industrial story published in 1910 under the auspices of the Birmingham Chamber of Commerce. She pronounced him "the strongest force in the industrial history of Alabama."

This ardent advocate of exploiting the cheap raw materials and the cheap labor of the hill country was a faithful servant of the absentee owners of the L. and N. Funds for his program came from the North and from Europe, as he put millions into expansions around Birmingham. His handiwork attracted attention in Wall Street, where journals like the *Commercial* and *Financial Chronicle* praised the railroad development in the Alabama mineral area. But he was primarily a railroader, not a captain of high finance. If control of his company was taken over by the Atlantic Coast Line, in 1902, the arrangement was engineered by a Morgan group, and it was astonishing news to Milton Hannibal Smith.

The hard-boiled manager, whose personal influence reached every brakeman on the L. and N., was as powerless to prevent extravagant booms on Main Street as to prevent speculative raids on his system on Wall Street. The mining development sent a speculative fever throughout the up-country of Alabama, Georgia, and Tennessee, especially in days of prosperity. The most conspicuous examples of "booms" and "busts" were perhaps at places in De Kalb County, Alabama, along the railroad between Birmingham and Chattanooga, about 1890. One of these "boom towns" was Fort Payne, where a coal and iron company was organized, with a million dollars raised in New England for the project. Two blast furnaces and a steel plant were constructed, but only to be dismantled and sold for scrap without ever being operated. Hundreds of little investors lost savings in the venture. Tallapoosa, in Georgia, had a boom in land sales, business development, and social life, with excursions of prominent visitors from New York and elsewhere. Spacious hotels sprang up in various hill villages and often proved too large for future use. Such a hotel building at Tecumseh, with its hand-carved finishings, was torn down during the second World War to furnish material for a campground church at the near-by village of Pleasant Gap. The passing of hand and wagon methods of mining iron ore flattened the Tecumseh land boom and reduced the town to the status of a railway flag station.

In flush times amateur prospectors and pseudo-geologists roamed the hillsides, sometimes getting free meals and lodgings from farmers who had hopes of finding iron ore on their lands or of selling what they had already found. I knew a traveler to give up his combination Punch and Judy show and photographic tent and settle down for several months at the job of getting out ore for others, who went broke. Three ex-slave families in my community sold their homesteads back in the woods for neat gains to mining speculators. Country merchants got in the game, either on their own account or as agents for others, in one case for a Cincinnati purchaser. Then there were quarries and kilns to supply lime to the iron works. As certain of the furnaces continued to use charcoal for decades after the Civil War, farmers sold wood to collieries or stacked wood in conical-shaped piles, covered it with dirt, and burnt it into coal themselves. Local sawmilling increased, and many hewed and cut cross-ties for the new railroads and spur tracks. These various activities were called "public works" in farm communities, and "public works" were spreading through the hills.

More important than coal and iron for the industrial awakening of the whole Piedmont area was cotton milling. This business was known to the antebellum South. It was based on the region's chief crop, and cotton was still king. Much of the up-country, like the rest of the South, was cotton conscious. Textile mills could be operated successfully on a smaller scale than iron and steel plants, and, therefore, were less dependent upon outside capital. It was recognized that after the Civil War Southern cotton mills paid high dividends, sometimes in fabulous figures. The hill country had a growing mass of white workers needing employment, workers who could at least tend machinery for making simple yarn and coarse cloth. Commission houses in the North wanted to handle the products, and manufacturers of mill machinery were anxious to find new buyers. Even second-hand machinery came south. Around 1880 and in the following years the daily and weekly press throughout the hill country carried on a campaign for cotton mills. Henry Grady and his Atlanta *Constitution* took up the cause, which Carolina editors had been supporting for some years. Every town and village wanted a mill for reasons of profits, payrolls, and philanthropy. That was the way of "real reconstruction," of economic emancipation for the New South. It was urged that factories be established "where the cotton grows up to the doorsteps of your mills, and supply and demand clasp hands."

This textile industry was featured at the Atlanta International Cotton Exposition, which was held in 1881 and which illustrated all phases of the cotton system from field to mill. The project was widely supported in both South and North, and General Sherman subscribed two thousand dollars to make it a success. A group of New Englanders participated. Many exhibits were sold and extensive orders were taken for machinery. In the following year two cotton factories were started in Atlanta, one of them in the exhibition building. A cotton compress and a cottonseed oil mill were established, and other new enterprises pushed Atlanta on the way, in tune with the quickening energies of the times. A Georgia spokesman at the Exposition of 1881 emphasized that the old "fabric of thought and of habit" was yielding to "a new era of progressive enterprise."

The rise of the cottonseed oil industry in this period supplied an additional link between farming and manufac-

turing in the cotton belt. The hill country had its share of
this industry, which brought a little more cash to cotton
farmers and ginners, furnished new feeds for cattle and logging oxen, offered new sources of elements for commercial
fertilizer, and provided oil for oleomargarine and for syn-
thetic lard. The new human foods provoked bitter political
controversies between the cotton country and the country
where dairying and hog-raising were important. Joe Wheeler
and others spoke in Congress for cottonseed and chemistry
and against restrictive taxation. "Compound lard" was saved,
but the dairymen got their tax on the "poor man's butter."
Use of cottonseed products expanded, and many of the hill
cities soon had "oil mills," with their early-morning whistle
during the harvest season. In my boyhood days on the farm
we could haul cotton a few miles up the road and sell it
to a cotton factory, and we could haul cottonseed a few
miles down the road and sell it to an "oil mill." We were
in walking distance of the Industrial Revolution, and country boys had feelings that things were happening.

Into the center of this changing economic picture moved
Henry W. Grady, who became the chief spokesman of the
New South before his death at thirty-nine. He was a product
of the hill country, the son of a prosperous merchant and
real estate owner of Athens, Georgia. This merchant was
reluctant for secession and supported the Unionist, Bell, for
President in 1860. He became a Confederate captain and
died of wounds, leaving his family in comfortable circumstances. Too young for war service, Henry later attended
the state universities of Georgia and Virginia, delivering a
senior oration on "Air Castles." He turned immediately to

49

journalism, and, as a reporter, he covered a special press excursion to industrial points along the railroad from Atlanta to Chattanooga. He settled down at the age of nineteen for three years on Rome papers, returning to Atlanta for a short series of publishing failures and service as correspondent for the New York *Herald.* Then for the rest of his life he was on the staff of the Atlanta *Constitution,* which had been established in 1868 to support "constitutional government" and the Andrew Johnson policy of Reconstruction.

Grady in 1880 made a journey to the northern reaches of the L. and N. lines and on to New York in company with H. V. Newcomb, vice president of that road. In New York he borrowed twenty thousand dollars from the financier, Cyrus W. Field, to purchase a fourth interest in the *Constitution,* at the same time arranging to buy L. and N. stock on margins and on Newcomb's advice, so as to repay the loan speedily. This increased his status as editor of the largest paper in the Lower Piedmont Country, where the Birmingham *Age-Herald* and Adolph S. Ochs' Chattanooga *Times* were among regional "contemporaries."

Grady was well equipped to champion the cause of progress, while Milton Smith was building rail lines and calling for freight. He was a master of words. In college he had an aversion for science and mathematics, but he became saturated with the writings and sentiments of Dickens, to whom he likened Bret Harte. He admired the showmanship of P. T. Barnum, whose autobiography he thoroughly absorbed. He could write news, and he could make news. He could devise scoops, and he could turn out human-interest feature stories. Under his managerial editorship, the Atlanta *Con-*

stitution became an up-country institution, especially through the wide rural circulation of its weekly edition. At places like Possum Trot it was the last word on the topics of the times. I speak from experience in a rural post office, where I took subscriptions for the *Weekly Constitution* at a dollar a year, retaining twenty-five cents as agent's commission.

The editor and his paper naturally boosted the International Cotton Exposition of 1881 as well as the subsequent fairs and expositions held in Atlanta. They popularized and dramatized the big idea of progress for Atlanta and the South.

Grady's recent biographer, Raymond B. Nixon, notes that he began editorial use of the term "New South" at least as early as March 14, 1874, in endorsing a plan to build Atlanta's first cotton mill by public subscription and favoring a proposal to make the able carpet-bagger, H. I. Kimball, its first president. For the next fifteen years of his life he made constant and consistent use of the words and the idea, fully justifying the biographical title, *Henry W. Grady: Spokesman of the New South*.

What did Grady mean by "New South"? This question is covered in the Nixon biography. He, of course, emphasized industrial growth as part of the meaning, appealing for both Southern and Northern capital to foster this development. He was not disturbed by complaints by the Chattanooga *Times* in 1887 that three-fifths of the new capital was coming from the North and that this boded ill for the South. He optimistically assumed that Southern "brains and enterprise" would handle the capital in ways that would be beneficial. This joint effort for the South was, in his eyes, the way to end sectional politics and turn the bitterness of the Civil War into a tender memory. He wanted a diversified type of farming, and he lamented the one-crop tenant system. He advocated economic and educational opportunities for Negroes within the pattern of segregation.

Grady gave the essentials of his magic formula to the New England Society at Delmonico's in New York in 1886. Following General Sherman on the program, he responded to the toast, "The New South." In glorifying the New South, he did not repudiate the Old South, but said it was dead except in a sentimental sense. He dealt with the past in terms of Dickens, with the future in terms of a Chamber of Commerce booster. The next day he could, like Lord Byron, have said that he waked up famous. His twenty-minute speech was widely acclaimed in his own up-country and in Wall Street. Clearly the New South was on the way, with Grady as its chief lay statesman. When he died of pneumonia three years later just after bringing a Boston audience to tears on "The Race Problem in the South," he was mourned in high places and low. News of his death practically broke up the progress of a dance at the antebellum town of Jacksonville, Alabama. It was said of him that he died "loving a nation into peace." The early passing of this man of the hour prevented him from witnessing the panic and industrial stagnation of the nineties, the climax of the farmers' revolt, and later an Atlanta race riot that rocked the New South. But his brief career made a permanent impact on the outlook of the up-country. To the dominant groups of that country of short history, short traditions, and short convictions he helped give a spirit of industrial enterprise that broke forever with the agrarian notions of the Old South.

4

Small Farms and Country Stores

THE HILL COUNTRY, with all its expansion of mines and mills, was far from a high stage of industrialization when obituary tributes were paid to Grady or even to Milton Smith. Industrial activity was important in the economic life of the region, and many a plowboy hoped to grow up and say farewell to the farm. In the rural school which I attended there were boys who aspired to become railway trainmen, as some of them did. There were others who wanted jobs with lumber companies, with urban mercantile establishments, or in cotton mills. Not infrequently parents, especially mothers, observed that they were not raising their boys to be farmers or their girls to be farm wives. Yet farming remained the main way of life for the majority. Much of the urban business of the hills consisted of selling merchandise to farm families, buying farm products, and providing credit for farm operations. Farms furnished or received much of the freight which moved over the new railroads.

After the Civil War, sharecropping and other forms of

share tenancy spread into portions of the hill country, supplanting slavery, as in the low country. This was especially true of areas of good lands which were easily accessible to rail or river traffic. The uplands, since pioneer days, however, have had many small farms cultivated by their owners. Some of these farms, especially in the mountainous backwoods, have grown more products for home consumption than for sale. The march of time has reduced the amount of successful subsistence farming by sturdy yeomen, though depression periods have forced poor people back to poor lands for a scanty existence, sometimes by plowing oxen.

With a high proportion of white farmers and a small proportion of plantations, the up-country has escaped much of the darker phase of sharecropping, such as has characterized the black belts of Alabama and Georgia or the Mississippi-Arkansas Delta regions. Many of its farm tenants have been, not sharecroppers working "on halves," but share-tenants, owning their own livestock and farm equipment and farming on a "third and fourth" basis, which means paying the landlord one-third of the grain and hay and one-fourth of the cotton. It was also true up to the first World War that the up-country had less absentee landlordism than these other regions. In many instances, the landlord in the hills lived on his farm near his tenants, making a crop himself and keeping in contact with his renters in an advisory or supervisory capacity. Because of these circumstances as well as a wide use of commercial fertilizer, the industrial up-country has often led the Alabama-Georgia lowlands in farm production, whether measured by the acre or by the man, white or colored. Its minority of Negro farmers have farmed better and fared better than Negro farmer majorities in other regions, at least, as long as they could remain on the land.

The hill country far surpassed the black belt country in the expansion of cotton production in the years after the Civil War when this crop was expanding. Cotton from surrounding farms has contributed heavily to the development of such market centers as Rome, Cedartown, Gadsden, and Anniston.

This expansion, besides providing greater sales of cotton and cottonseed, meant greater purchases by farmers. It brought in carloads or droves of mules from Missouri, Kentucky, and Tennessee. It brought in one-horse and two-horse farm wagons, including many of the Studebaker make, which a hillbilly once called for under the name of "Rutabaga." It built up a substantial industry in the mixing of fertilizer, which farmers bought by the ton "to raise more cotton to pay more debts." It increased the purchase of flour and side-meat from the Middle West. It increased the occasions of farmers' "going to town to buy some more corn to raise some more cotton to buy some more corn" and so on in a vicious cycle. Incidentally the cotton expansion meant the clearing of trees from thousands of hills, with much of the wood burned on the spot and with no providing of terraces or winter cover-crops to check the destructive forces of erosion. Asked why he did not do something toward saving his soil, the owner of several hundred acres frankly assured me that he could buy additional land more cheaply than he could terrace what he had. Indebted farmers and tenants had little choice but to mine the soil for immediate gain, with little thought of the future, which was to see more abandoned acres in their hills than in any other comparable area of America.

Closer to these farmers than the city factors and financiers were the village merchants and the crossroads storekeepers. These pillars of rural society increased in numbers and importance with the collapse of the slave economy and with the expansion of farming after the Civil War. Like the cowboys of the West, they played an important role for an era and then yielded largely to new ways and new times. The country store was to last longer as a real institution in the South than in other regions.

The rural dealers who opened up stores in the hills after "the surrender" varied widely in power, standing, and business methods. Practically all made use of mortgages and crop liens in extending credit to their customers. The crop lien, well legalized in Reconstruction times, developed along with the Southern farm tenant system. Both systems developed for the reason that the farm owners lacked operating funds, either for wages or for current supplies. Sometimes the landlord was his own merchant and automatically had a lien on the crops of his tenants. He, in turn, would have to get credit, perhaps through lien notes. Often the landlord "stood security" for his tenants or waived his lien in favor of a local merchant.

There were pretentious merchants who went to the happy hunting grounds of New York for credit and capital in the Reconstruction period. Many years ago I interviewed a retired and wealthy merchant of this class. In his active years he carried a bank account in New York, for there was no bank at his place or near it. He bought cotton from his farm customers and sold it through a New York house, thus replenishing his distant bank deposits. He issued checks and cashed checks for others, charging a fee either way. He "furnished" farmers "on time" for fall payment for the merchandise, and he made the indebtedness secure by taking crop liens, chattel mortgages, and even land mortgages. His prices were high, and his sales were large, for his "time" customers could not shop around among competitors. His name was Walt Dean, and a folk rhyme linked it with lien (called "lean") to suggest two features not to be found in Heaven. In the end this country-town merchant became the owner of many farms and other properties. By hill standards he was "big rich."

More typical of the ways of rural commerce in the uplands was the country-store career of Bill Nixon, my father, who operated on a smaller scale than Dean. Starting in 1885, he conducted a store for forty years at Merrellton, Alabama, a Southern Railway flag station forty-seven miles southwest of Rome, near a neighborhood unofficially designated as Possum Trot. He began with a cash capital of two hundred and fifty dollars, which he had saved from four years of teaching one-room schools. He had to borrow money and, in the beginning years, he had to pay an annual interest of seventeen per cent. He made money while borrowing at that rate, and he certainly charged his customers more than seventeen per cent above cash prices for goods sold "on time" for autumn payment. He mastered and practiced the priority principles of crop liens. He combined farming with merchandising as business gains enabled him to acquire lands. Thus he had for years an approximate monopoly of sales to his own tenants and croppers. He got a share of each crop for rent, and then got a store account payment out of the tenant's share. Since the account was marked up, he got interest as well as profit and rent returns out of the accumulative process. Acquisition of a grist mill and cotton gin brought additional toll from tenants and other customers, with steady profits through purchases of cottonseed for sale to oil mills.

There was constant watching to make sure that tenants' accounts did not run ahead of their crop work and crop prospects. A tenant, getting in a risky situation, might be told to speed up his work or to cut down on his buying. In certain cases, purchases would be limited to food, tobacco, and absolutely necessary work clothes. To head off criticism, a particular cropper, whose account was being held down one year, adopted the practice of stating his need in requesting a purchase. "I want a pair of pants for Bill," he once said, "He's entirely out." There were also precautions to prevent tenants and customers from "beating their accounts" in the fall. One share tenant, undertaking to dispose of cotton in a neighboring town without putting it on his debt, was overtaken by a bailiff with attachment papers and saw his cotton unloaded by the side of the road. A debtor, who planned to move to Texas without paying his store account, found his household effects attached on the way to the railroad station, making payment necessary before shipment out of the state.

This store, like many others in the hill country, had other business besides furnishing farmers for autumn payment. There was an industrial spirit about the place, in spite of the rural comment and the aroma from open barrels and boxes of sugar, coffee, candy, and chewing tobacco. There were customers who paid cash or paid up by the month. Among these were members of railway "section gangs," wood-choppers, sawmill workers, cross-tie cutters, employees of a rock quarry, iron ore workers and haulers at times, and, for some years, men who came from a distillery on the other side of the creek. Railway trainmen purchased chickens and eggs, which had been received from farm families "in trade."

The local post office, established in one corner of the store, furnished additional activity and importance to the day's work. Drummers came frequently, with samples of their lines of dry goods, notions, shoes, patent medicines, pocket knives, tobacco, and other items, including jokes, both old and new. They came by train and by horse and buggy until the automobile became their sole means of travel. Sometimes they ate fried chicken as paying guests in the storekeeper's home.

Such a place in its prime was a neighborhood center and also the headquarters for the varied operations of the owner, who left much of the routine of selling goods across the counter to a hired "clerk" or to members of his family. Customers' accounts included, not only store purchases, but charges for other things, such as meal from the mill, corn from the crib, rent for a spare house, a pig from the barn, or the service of a bull. Sometimes a slow tenant's crop was worked out by hired help, with the wages charged to his account. In the period when William Jennings Bryan was preaching free silver, Bill Nixon occasionally made a simple plank coffin and charged it to a tenant or customer who lacked the cash or crop credit to provide other ways for the burial of a deceased member of his family.

Merchants like Nixon were thus always on the go, and practically every move was connected with the seeking of gain. They had little time for either religion or pleasure, though their chasing of dollars became a sort of mixture of religion and pleasure. Many of them avoided whiskey and controversial politics, though there were exceptions on both counts. Clem Reid, when a partner in a store two miles from Nixon's place, was once left in sole charge by the other partner, who went away for a few days. As the partner returned and found the business neglected, he asked, "Clem, how long have you been drunk?"

Clem replied, "Yesterday, today, and tomorrow."

When Bluffton, Alabama, was a prosperous crossroads iron center, a local merchant acquired the nickname of "Bell Tree" for his manner of handling whiskey illegally on the side. The customer would put his purchase money in a box under a tree a short distance from the store, ring a bell that was attached to the tree, and immediately disappear down the road. Upon hearing the bell sound again, he would return to the tree, find his whiskey instead of money in the box, and depart without ever seeing a salesman, as if he had patronized a mechanical automat.

It seemed wise to many rural merchants to practice tact and patience when the agrarian crusade hit the hill country in the years before and after 1890. Sidney Lanier had said in 1880 that the "New South means small farming," but even Henry Grady was soon to observe that throughout the South merchants were prosperous and farmers were poor.

As the Farmers' Alliance movement and the Populist movement got under way, hill farmers went on the political warpath, denouncing all types of monopolists and middle-men along the way. There were complaints about high interest rates and high prices that farmers had to pay. Railroad freight rates were denounced as exorbitant and discriminatory. Critics did not limit themselves to attacking trusts and "robber barons" of Wall Street but also gave attention to bankers, merchants, and landlords of Main Street. Redress was sought through cooperative merchandise exchanges and through regulatory legislation. Country storekeepers frequently sympathized with the farmers' analysis of national ills, stuck to business, and saw the cooperatives fail or fold up. At the same time a number of merchants went broke through the inability of destitute customers to pay their accounts, with farm products at panic prices.

The up-country was full of farmers' rallies for reform. The most prominent leaders of the "woolhat boys" in this campaign to overthrow the "bourbons" were Thomas E. Watson of Georgia and Reuben F. Kolb of Alabama, both from old regions below the hills. But the hill country furnished its own champion reformer in William H. Felton, of Cartersville, Georgia. He was simultaneously a farmer, Methodist preacher, and country physician. He fought the regular Democratic machine of his state and went to Congress as an Independent, serving three terms. He opposed the convict lease system of Georgia and saw it abolished some years ahead of such a change in Alabama. His chief supporter was his wife, Rebecca Latimer Felton, a progressive leader and speaker, who for thirty years aired her views in the columns of the Atlanta *Journal,* which took leanings toward reform and "covered Georgia like the dew." Near the end of her life of ninety-five years, Mrs. Felton by appointment served a short time in the United States Senate, furnishing a fitting finish to the career of a Southern suffragette from the hills.

Moved by the politics of poverty, the small farmers of the uplands, as of other sections, gave strong support to the agrarian crusade. They heeded the words of reform leaders within the Democratic Party, and many went over to the new Populist Party. They started a campaign, which sooner or later, brought on stricter regulation of the railroads. But, as in antebellum times, they found themselves opposed by powerful planter politicians of the black belts, now reinforced by the corporations which had developed in the Piedmont region. The conservative leaders controlled the Negro vote, stuffed ballot boxes, and manipulated the election returns in various ways to prevent the "damn Populists from ruining the country." Reuben F. Kolb, candidate for governor of Alabama in 1892, with the support of the Populist and the Farmers' Alliance, was very likely defeated by a dishonest count, not by an honest vote. Many precincts reported more votes against him than were physically possible. Years later a South Alabama election official told me that he was a party to returning one thousand five hundred Kolb votes as anti-Kolb votes. The conservative legislature and governor could or would do nothing to investigate matters. In this critical period, there was talk of violence, of bayonets and blood. There were heavy sales of firearms, including pistols.

But the progressives had appealed to the Negroes, whose votes the conservatives had succeeded in corralling to supply the balance of power. Republicans had also entered the picture against the regular organizations of the Democratic Party. The continued control of Negro voters by planter bourbons was precarious, and the Democratic Party's solid South was threatened with another era of Reconstruction. The result was a series of constitutional and legislative changes in the South to bar most of the Negroes from registering for voting and to provide a poll tax as an additional requirement for voting.

The hill farmers, like Patrick Henry a century earlier, smelled a rat and frequently opposed the steps toward a smaller electorate. But, again, they were outvoted, especially in counties where manipulated Negro votes swelled majorities for disfranchisement. This was exemplified in the campaign for ratification of the Alabama constitution of 1901 with its various limitations on voting. The advocates of ratification emphasized Negro disfranchisement and disclaimed white disfranchisement. There was a temporary "grandfather clause," and "no white man will be disfranchised." Yet most of the white counties voted against it, while important black belt counties voted heavily for it. Decisive majorities for ratification came from lowland counties lacking white voters to furnish those majorities. In some mysterious way Negroes voted heavily to deny themselves the suffrage and incidentally to reduce the white vote. White registration was then a mere matter of routine, but a rigid application of educational and other tests headed off the Negroes. In time the poll tax requirement resulted in more whites than Negroes going without the vote. The hillbillies' suspicions were confirmed.

Farmers' Alliance banners gathered dust in attics.

Populism, Bryan, and free silver were forgotten with the coming of better times at the turn of the century. Political gatherings, speakings, and barbecues became less frequent on the countryside with the decline in the proportion of voters. Farm tenancy increased, and many of the best lands were consolidated into large holdings, frequently under absentee landlords. Many of the owners preferred to avoid share-croppers and to have tenants who required less supervision. Some of these tenants, in turn, rented small crops to share-croppers. With a high birth rate, individuals and families were constantly leaving or seeking to leave the hill farms. They migrated to towns and cities of the up-country. They moved to Florida, Oklahoma, and Texas. A number of families in and around Farmersville, Texas, can trace ances-try back to a rural family burial ground in Northeast Ala-bama. In good times hill people moved to Detroit, Chicago, and other distant places for industrial employment.

Hill farmers, by choice or necessity, moved considerably away from excessive reliance on cotton production after the first World War. They could not fight the boll weevil scien-tifically and mechanically on a wide scale as could the farm-ers of the Delta and the Great Plains. They found in the panic following 1920 that they could not eat their cotton, which had lost its market. They again discovered this fact in the "Hoover depression," which one hillbilly called a "compression." In different ways the New Deal farm program and both World Wars stimulated a diversified agriculture and more food production. These changes saw many share-croppers leave the farm, as the power of cotton declined, while hay farming and cattle raising expanded.

The country store lost much of its community significance with the coming of automobiles, good roads, and closer contact between town and country. It became more dependent upon the highway than upon the railroad for transportation, with complete abandonment of Coosa River steamboat traffic. It lost its monopoly of neighborhood farm trade as country customers found their way to general stores and chain stores in town. It picked up more trade from people passing by. Store locations changed. So did the line of merchandise. Country merchants continued to carry staple groceries and hardware and a few drugs, but they gave less attention to such items as cologne, corsets, lace, general dry goods, Christmas toys, and wide varieties of patent medicines. Gasoline service pumps appeared in front of many country stores, and new stores were established to supplement service stations. Soft drink sales increased, and a sprinkling of establishments sprang up for the sale of beer and meals or sandwiches along the roadside. This meant less reliance by rural travellers or loafers upon soda crackers and canned goods, such as sardines, salmon, and oysters, with pepper sauce, foods which I served across the counter for years to members of both races, with three soup bowls and three spoons to facilitate the selling and serving. Striped stick candy no longer came in by the barrel. It yielded largely to candy bars.

The crop-lien credit business of country stores declined with the growth of country banks, the providing of different forms of government credit for farmers, and the decrease in the number of rural cotton gins. The proportion of cash sales increased and the autumn rush of collections became largely a practice of the past. Gone were many of the risks, gains, and losses in furnishing farmers on time.

The country store shifted from a dominant position to a routine place in the rural economy of the hills, though continuing to bring in profits at strategic locations, especially in properous times. A good number of old-line storekeepers and their sons moved into other activities, becoming Main Street bankers, wholesale grocers, managers of urban ginning establishments, warehousemen, cotton merchants, independent planters, lumbermen, real-estate dealers, and the like. Some became directors of cotton mills and in time took in dividends that doubled or trebled original investments. That was before King Cotton got sick. Storekeeper families have furnished many members to the professions, especially women schoolteachers. There are examples of women in the hills operating country stores in their own name. They did not wait for wartime to succeed their men folk.

The country store of the hills, like the hill farm, is not what it used to be many years ago. It no longer fits the composite description given by Thomas D. Clark in *Pills, Petticoats, and Plows,* a book on the Southern country store between 1865 and 1915. It has lost its cracker box and its cracker-box philosophy. It has taken on more package merchandise and more standardized methods. In many ways there has been a shrinkage in the distance and the difference between rural and urban stores in the industrial up-country.

5

Cities and Towns

===

THE SOUTHERN hill country, thanks to its industries, is more urban than the low country. Having developed largely since the Civil War and with extensive financial aid from the North, the cities and towns of the uplands are more Yankeefied in tone and outlook than the older centers of the lowlands. Atlanta is more like New York than it is like Charleston. Birmingham is more like Pittsburgh than it is like Mobile or Montgomery. Chattanooga is more like Chicago than it is like Memphis. These major urban centers of the up-country, for instance, voted heavily for Hoover in 1928, while their sister cities of the low country, consistently cast majorities for Al Smith, though there was little difference between uplands and lowlands in the crucial issues of liquor and religion. The Old South centers stuck to political traditions. The New South centers, with an industrial consciousness, broke over to the Great Engineer of progress, prosperity, and the abolition of poverty, not seeing the panic around the corner.

Lower Piedmont Country

The Piedmont country is a region of expanding cities and receding frontier corners or pockets. Between the extremes of city and frontier are towns, industrial villages, and open-valley farm districts. In the material and superficial aspects of life urban standards are dominant. In fact, the region might be called the "ABC Country" in recognition of the influence of Atlanta, Birmingham, and Chattanooga in industry, commerce, finance, press, radio, and sports, whether amateur, professional, or collegiate. Rome citizens start the day and end it with newspapers just out of Atlanta and Chattanooga. Anniston readers get papers from Atlanta and Birmingham while the news is fresh. Every town in this area reads dailies from two or three of the ABC cities, and sees its own doings, its murders and prominent weddings, reported with appropriate photographs in these papers. Negroes have an Atlanta daily, the *World*, and a Birmingham paper bearing the same name.

The ABC cities have been great places for hill people to visit and see the world. Before the days of automobiles and highways they were destination points for popular railway excursions. It seemed wonderful to ride a "Chattanoogy choo-choo," and a sad song said,

> *Write me a letter, send it by mail,*
> *Send it in care of Birmin'ham jail.*

The three cities have also been great centers of employment for the region. They set the pace for progress and furnish weather signals for the coming of good and bad times. Birmingham, being closely dependent on coal and iron industries, shows significant ups and downs in business and employment as the nation alternates between boom times and depressions. Few cities have products that are wanted more in periods of prosperity and less in periods of panic. George Leighton has a chapter on this "City of Perpetual Promise," in *America's Growing Pains,* his book on *The Romance, Comedy and Tragedy of Five Great Cities.* At the head of this chapter he quotes an old Birmingham adage, "Hard times come here first and stay longest." The city had more than its share of neglected shacks, idle plants, and vacant business houses between 1930 and 1935. But production for the war against Hitler and Tojo put business into high gear again and brought back meaning to "Magic City" on the street sign in front of Birmingham's Terminal Station.

Atlanta leads Birmingham in white-collar trades and as a regional center for conventions, marketing farm mules, distributing Sears Roebuck merchandise, and administering various activities of the United States government. It has headquarters offices for the Southern activities of numerous organizations, including the American Federation of Labor, the CIO, and labor or racial groups. A cluster of colleges makes it the Athens of the South for Negroes. On the business side, Chattanooga is a cross between Atlanta and Birmingham, with the addition of being a mountain city on the Tennessee River. Its scenic and recreational resources are enhanced by near-by Chickamauga Lake, which was made by a TVA dam. Like Atlanta, it has the markings and memories of Civil War fighting, on which historical novels have been written.

Coming next in urban rank are half a dozen cities with a

total population running above a hundred and fifty thousand. These and the smaller cities or towns show more variety in background and development than the big three. Rome, Talladega, and Huntsville have a history extending back into stagecoach days. The last would be Twickenham, had not the War of 1812 caused its pioneers to drop the name of the home of Alexander Pope, the British poet, for their Tennessee Valley settlement. Instead they honored their own founder, John Hunt, and later the poet's home was used in other ways, as in furnishing the name for a cafe. The town soon became a cotton-market center and then also a cotton-mill town. It had closer ties with Nashville than with South Alabama in antebellum times. Rome, at the head of the Coosa River, got its start as a farm-market center, and, like Huntsville, can point to old homes and plantation architecture. It honors the name of General Forrest in various ways and for good reasons.

Anniston and Bessemer are examples of newer cities which got their start when railroads penetrated the Birmingham district. Anniston boasts that the products of its pipe foundries go all over the world and make it the leading center for this industry. Bessemer is virtually a corner of Birmingham, being separated by a few legal barriers and roadside juke boxes.

The Alabama towns of Jacksonville and Piedmont, just a dozen miles apart, contrast the Old and the New South, as though the former were in the black belt and the latter in Western Pennsylvania. Jacksonville, with its central square and half-dozen columned mansions, could once boast of a list of Confederate army officers, including captains, majors, a colonel or two, and a general. Its cemetery contains the grave of Captain John Pelham, "the gallant Pelham" in one of Robert E. Lee's reports. A rural ne'er-do-well once came to town, got drunk, and slept in an alley between the mansions of two of the local celebrities. With a sense of humor and meaning he later remarked that he did not want to make either townsman mad by spending the night with the other, and, therefore, he compromised by spending the night between them. The town of Piedmont preceded the older neighbor several years in getting a cotton mill and a Yankee superintendent. It has honored the Old South tradition with a Dixie Hotel, which was established by Tyler Ledbetter, a tall and easy-going man, a tobacco chewer, who claimed, with good evidence, that he had been the ugliest soldier in the Confederate army. His house served the best meals between Atlanta and Birmingham, with plenty on the table and a daughter to play "Dixie" on the piano regularly in the evenings for the guests. When the mill superintendent asked for a change of the hotel name so he could patronize it, Ledbetter took the remark as an insult and responded accordingly.

Most of these towns and cities have each a weekly or daily paper. Some of the papers have been close to the soil and to the people in general outlook. A striking example was the Dahlonega, Georgia, *Nugget* during the life of its editor and publisher, W. B. Townsend. He transferred wise sayings and pointed comments directly from his brain to his type, sometimes going barefooted in the process, according to good newspaper accounts. In other cases rural correspondents, with a shortage of personal items for their town papers, would often try their hand at wit and humor. A frequent gag in springtime on the eve of primary elections used to be, "The farmers are afraid to cut down a tree for fear it would fall on a candidate."

Much of this press has been commercialized and standardized, occasionally with absentee ownership and with papers of two or three towns under the same control. This has brought a decline in personal journalism, in pointed editorials, such as in times past have involved Southern editors in duels. The publisher of a weekly in a growing town told me frankly that his paper should really have no editorials and take no side in local issues. An "independent" publisher in a larger center said that, if he should write as he pleased on a utility issue, his banker would be on his neck. Another publisher got "in Dutch" with his civic club for showing labor sympathy during a textile strike some years ago.

The New Deal restored an element of diversity in the hill country press by provoking strong opposition, attracting strong support, and stimulating several papers to adopt a critical middle-of-the-road policy. The late W. S. Mudd, owner of newspapers and other properties in Rome, Gadsden, and elsewhere, expanded his broadside against the New Deal into a book *The Old Boat Rocker*. On the other side of the fence was the Anniston *Star*, which had been pro-Wilson in President Wilson's time and after, and consistently supported the Roosevelt program for four terms.

The typical industrial town of the hill country has at least three groups or sections, not just two divided by a railroad track. Sometimes the sections have taken on such local names as "Milltown," "Uptown," and "Niggertown." During hard times prior to 1900 one town's Negro section become "Needmore." The threefold classification could be applied generally to people, homes, schools, churches, business, and other activities. White workers in cotton mills have been set off to themselves about as definitely as the Negroes, whose connection with the mills since the Civil War has been limited to common labor employment, such as unloading incoming bales of cotton. In fact, the mill section has often been the most compact unit of the town, though a portion of the workers might be coming in daily from rural homes. There have been exceptions to this pattern, as in cases of mill families using the same school or church as others, especially when higher wages came into the picture. Baseball games have brought mill employees and other people together. But those who work in the mill have been pretty conscious of a social barrier separating them from "Uptown" and have also been insistent on a barrier between themselves and the Negroes. In turn, the Negroes have been alert to recognize the barrier between whites and whites, as in the period of slavery.

The race relations and the labor relations of the industrial towns have a rural background. Laborers and labor attitudes came, in the first place, from the Southern countryside. So did many of the employers, and the Northern employers, coming South, generally adjusted themselves to the Southern pattern. In a measure the cotton mill reproduced the labor picture of the tenant plantation, which in its early stages continued the paternalistic idea of master and slaves. The lord of the mill was much like the lord of the plantation, and his labor supply was drawn largely from farm tenant groups and other farm families whose level of living was low. The workers generally became tenants in company houses just as they had been tenants in houses of the rural landlord. The same system of dependency prevailed, and, with it, little sense of civic responsibility on the part of those who toiled at manual labor. After all, hand work for wages was not quite dignified or respectable, especially for women.

These native white workers from foothills and mountain country have been praised for their individualism and their slowness to join or form labor unions. A. B. Moore in his *History of Alabama* (published in 1934) says they are "psychologically fit" for the textile industry, being "industrious, reliable, responsive, practical-minded and possessed of the power of gratitude," and he points with pride to "their satisfaction with working conditions" and their comparative immunity to trade unionism. Conditions have subsequently changed, but Moore's brief words are true of the cheap labor in the Piedmont textile industry from the Civil War to the New Deal. His estimate of labor in the hill country had been emphasized by others, including Chambers of Commerce. Circulars for promoting textile mills had used such language as "abundance of competent labor of Anglo-Saxon extraction." The *Manufacturer's Record* of Baltimore, noting the growth of the textile industry in the South, praised the region for being free from "anarchistic labor leaders."

This rural-made set of labor relations often included friendly contacts between employer and employees, and there were mill officials who took a personal and paternalistic interest in the general welfare of their workers. When unions and strikes came to the mills, it was hard for these officials to understand how their personally supervised workers could or would turn against benevolent employers. One superintendent talked to me in 1935 about a strike, almost with tears in his eyes. In his way of thinking he had met with colossal human ingratitude, and he was disillusioned.

Workers in times past have appreciated the paternalistic view and have found the company store a good institution for keeping them out of the clutches of loan sharks and free from those creditors' attempts to attach their wages through garnishment proceedings. They have been glad to accept non-union wages, which have often seemed good in comparison with farm tenants' earnings. Workers and Southern writers have had good words about the sanitation, health, and welfare program of the United States Steel's Tennessee Company at Birmingham. There is praise for this in Edwin Mims' *Advancing South,* which appeared in the middle twenties as a liberal appraisal of the region.

It has not been easy for outside organizers to understand this attitude or to be, in turn, understood by the agrarian-minded workers who have moved from farm to mill. I once heard a woman worker say to an intellectual laborite, "You are not a worker and still would not be a worker if you used your hands a hundred and fifty years." Unionized workers have often found themselves misunderstood or opposed by their rural relatives. Picket lines have seemed odd to rural customers coming to town to trade, as I have witnessed in wartime Anniston. Farm tenants have said their in-laws and cousins in town were asking for too much in textile strikes. Speaking of relatives of Gadsden, a farm wife said,

"We don't discuss labor questions when they come to see us."

Industrial leaders have had important power and influence in the guidance and government of the hill country towns, much more than the rural-minded workers. This has been especially true of one-industry centers and of municipalities that gave tax reductions and other concessions to new factories. Like planters in the lowlands, these leaders have often had the main word in local government, school management, recreational activities, and civic clubs. As pointed out by Liston Pope in *Mill Hands and Preachers* and by others, they have supported churches and had something to say about the preachers who served the working classes. With strong local support, they have, in many instances, been in position to make labor unions seem unnecessary and to have no truck with outside "agitators," even through World War II.

There were symptoms, however, in many towns of the growing pains of the New South as industrial unionism sought to follow industrial capital into the hill country. There were cases of strikes without effective unionization or leadership, and these generally failed. Unions and strikes did not fit the rural patterns of the towns of the up-country.

In the thorny road to collective bargaining in the industrial centers Negro workers went through changing roles. Excluded from skilled trades and from unions for years, they were used for strike-breakers in certain heavy industries. They were so used in mines around Birmingham in the eighteen nineties, about the time the South and the nation were applauding Booker T. Washington's eloquent speech in Atlanta on harmonious race relations, mutual progress, and Southern economic opportunity for his people. Then by evolutionary stages and interracial adjustments they became regular members of unions and labor councils in the cities and industries in which their work and numbers were important. The transition is incomplete, and the roles remained mixed, but many Negroes take their union meetings and duties seriously. "If my bishop says anything against labor, he's wrong," insisted a Birmingham Negro preacher and worker to his union council.

The economic progress and the worship of industry in the up-country have not made the rank and file industrial-minded or urban-minded in any genuine sense. With few exceptions, every town or city is important for its farm trade and farmer contacts, and every county courthouse looks like a rural meeting place, inside and out. Rural influences have come to town with rural people. There has been a great tendency for members of upper-class and yeomen families to move from farm to town to engage in some type of white-collar business or occupation. This is explained partly by the lack of acquaintance in the rural South with technological careers or opportunities and partly by a handed-down tradition of lower status for manual laborers. At times a social virtue seems to attach to what a local wag called "wearing out trousers notwithstanding." These big and little men of business and professions retain much of the rural outlook, of individualism and conservatism. They are out of the country, but the country is not out of them. Old ways suit them.

The urban centers of the up-country have numerous persons who are members of no labor union, no civic club, no

Chamber of Commerce, no church, no organization of any kind, and have no vote. They have no sense of belonging. Largely of old Anglo-Saxon and African stock, they have no Old World folk culture to tie them together in little groups. They are native Americans stranded in America. They are in a community but not of it. Their vital contact with urban life is almost restricted to their roles as workers and spenders, aside from occasional business in police court or the county courthouse. They are to be found in the largest industrial city and in the smallest market town.

Nature and geography, however, favor the cities of the hills as locations that are suitable for human habitation. In the first place, good water is available without excessive effort or cost, though many an urban dwelling has no bath or inside toilet. An Alabama town, with its water supply coming by gravity through a pipe from a large spring on a nearby mountain, had a hot campaign for the election of mayor some years ago on the issue of whether to require cans to be placed under dry privies for hauling the refuse away regularly. The ticket slogans became "cans" and "anti-cans," the "cans" winning.

Big Spring, which Indian villagers originally used and named, furnishes Cedartown in Georgia its millions of gallons of water daily. Jacksonville, Alabama, is built around a big spring, with its flow from "Uptown" through "Milltown." Anniston gets its spring water from Coldwater a few miles away. Neither Cavespring, Rock Spring, Goodwater, nor any large city of this region should ever have any serious water problems.

The inhabitants of any town or city of this country can

see the sun rise and set over tree-covered hills or mountains. They can hear the whistle of railway trains moving among or alongside these ranges. They can escape to these high spots to avoid summer heat or reside the year round on a mountain drive, economic circumstances permitting. Birmingham has its Red Mountain overlooking that city and its sprawling industries. Chattanooga has Signal and Lookout, where suburbanites dwell and tourists buy postcard scenes of Civil War battles. Atlanta, with its thousand-foot elevation, is within eight miles of Stone Mountain, where sculptors have carved a massive head of Robert E. Lee and Ku Klux Klansmen have burned massive fiery crosses.

The towns and cities of this region are in a setting of natural surroundings suggestive of the scenery of Switzerland. They are developing an interest in the tourist and playground possibilities of these scenic lands, where the natives have always loved outdoor life. Anniston and Huntsville are interested in near-by state parks. Chattanooga pushes its tourist business and a general recreational development. Guntersville has discovered that a TVA lake means more income for the town than was lost from the flooding of farm lands on three sides. Sales of fishing tackle have replaced the market for farm equipment. Boatmakers have supplanted oldfashioned blacksmiths. There is an interest here and elsewhere in town planning, in removing portions of man-made ugliness.

In recreational interests the towns of the hill country are in the early or primary stages of development, as is also largely true of their industries and their surrounding agriculture. They have not yet got around to a strong emphasis on quality, on high-class services and high-class finished products. On this score they trail Switzerland and many other sections both in recreation and in industry. By a value test, a pushcart load of Swiss watches might be balanced against a trainload of freight produced in a town of the New South. The hill centers have relied too long and too much upon coarse products and poor restaurants.

6

Sam Jones and the Ol' Time Religion

THE MOST popular religious spokesman of the reconstructed
New South was Samuel Porter Jones, the "mountain evangelist," who, like Henry Grady, grew up in North Georgia
and spent his career in the hill country. The preacher and
the editor were contemporaries. Both made a wide appeal to
their region, and both won a wide following among their
people. Through extensive quotation by his fellows, Jones
was a preacher's preacher, just as Grady was an editor's
editor. Said a popular revivalist of North Alabama, "I didn't
get my religion in any theological cemetery. I got it by following Sam Jones."

If Grady failed to win a college election, got on a drunk,
and then turned from politics to journalism for a career,
becoming an advocate of temperance, Jones failed as a lawyer
because of heavy drinking and turned to the Methodist
ministry as a reformed drunkard. He lived up to a promise
made to his dying father, but, according to one of many
stories about him, he got his first vision and fear of hell one

night while "dead-drunk" outdoors with a close view of an iron furnace in full blast. This looked too much like the fire of Judgment for comfort. Sam went forth to preach a dynamic gospel of individual salvation and to win drunkards away from the road to a burning hell. "The only way to quit drinking is to quit," he urged as he cited his own example. There was business support for his crusade, sometimes for the avowed reason that it improved the regularity of employment in the new industries.

Sam Jones always put on a good show, often in a big tent and occasionally with special trains and low rates to bring in people from the hills to hear him. In his day railroads were forbidden by Georgia law to operate freight trains on Sunday, but they could haul passengers to his meetings. When he was holding forth in his home town of Cartersville, northwest of Atlanta, a little coal-carrying railroad would operate extra cars to bring passengers from Alabama points on Sunday and revert to coal transportation on Monday.

This Savonarola to hillbillies graduated from circuit rider to regional revivalist and then to the status of a national evangelist. He attracted a wide following by his militant fight against the sale and use of liquor, which was "a good thing in its place, but its place is in hell." That was about the whole content of his social gospel, aside from saving individual souls. He brought about permanent or temporary changes in the life of thousands. He was always an entertaining speaker, often making wisecracks at his audiences, such as "I photograph your ugliness, and you sit there and laugh at it." He was not too dignified to talk about money, for it took "grace, grit, and greenbacks to run a meeting." With the Lord furnishing the grace and Jones the grit, the congregation, by division of labor, must come through with the greenbacks.

Sam Jones took the language of the soil into the pulpit. He stirred sinners into readiness before calling them to repentance, in accord with his explanation, "I never kill hogs till I get the water hot." He praised religion but manifested the common man's distaste for creeds and theology, and he "would rather be in Heaven learning my ABC's than sitting in hell reading Greek."

In politics he would have been called a demagogue for the way he played on certain popular notions or prejudices. He sometimes shocked sensitive and cultivated people, including ministers, by an uncouth plainness of speech. He said, "Many a man imagines that he has got religion, when it's only a liver-complaint." He condemned dancing as "hugging set to music," and turned his wrath upon women who played cards. Farm tenants have treasured, repeated, and expanded his denunciations of "society" women in low-neck evening dresses. They have especially attributed to him pointed comment about a dinner visit with much feminine nakedness above the table, Sam adding that he "did not look under the table."

Sam Jones and his large congregation in tent or tabernacle constituted an urban continuation of the rural camp meeting, which Methodists and other Protestant groups founded and developed in backwoods America. In the opening years of the nineteenth century, Lorenzo Dow, a Connecticut Methodist, made various preaching tours between Canada and Florida, holding and establishing camp meetings and fulfilling "chains of appointments" arranged for him by presiding elders and others. Often accompanied by Peggy, his fervently religious wife, he traveled by boat, buggy, horseback, and on foot. He touched points in East Tennessee, the upper counties of Georgia, and different sections of Alabama. Under his revival preaching enthusiastic hearers shouted and at times were seized by the "jerks." On some of the camp grounds in the hill country, portions of saplings were left standing for shouters to "jerk by," as Dow himself mentions in his journal. This type of muscular response to the gospel has declined since Dow's time, but it has not disappeared. At a Negro service in the Birmingham city auditorium in 1944, I saw the preacher at the pulpit jerk himself into a state of collapse, while several jerking members of the audience had to be held by their comrades, one woman getting loose and rolling and twisting in the aisle.

The camp meeting became an institutional mixture of religion and recreation, of revival services and picnicking, with an abundance of food prepared for the occasion. It has been subjected to criticisms, including many which Dow cited and denied. One was that it gave too much opportunity for preaching by ignorant ministers. Another, often supported by farmers, was that it wasted time for many people who should have been at home at work. This criticism was often avoided by holding the meeting after crops were "laid by" and before harvesting began. There was also the objection that the camp meeting was not a decent place for ladies and that young people used the occasion for courting, often sitting in buggies instead of worshipping and getting themselves prayed for. This brought the cynical comment, which

I have heard in my day, that more souls were made than saved at such goings on. But the criticism did not end the camp meeting system, which has served rural people down into the present century, partly yielding to new urban methods and other attractions. Many grounds have been abandoned, as at Peaceburg, between Anniston and the Coosa River, where the United States Army established an artillery range in the second World War. The thunder of cannon replaced the thunder of the sermon.

Many rural revivals have had just about all the features of a camp meeting, except the camping. In the hill country they generally take place in the slack farm season of late July and August. Visitors used to come to the evening services from a radius of miles, on foot and horseback, in buggies and farm wagons. To accommodate evening crowds too large for the church building, "bush arbors" were sometimes provided by placing tree tops or leafy limbs over a supporting structure of poles, with the ground for floor and maybe a covering of sawdust around the altar or "mourners' bench." This covered space might be inadequate, if great numbers "hit the sawdust trail." The subsequent baptizing into the church was a great occasion, particularly in the case of Baptists, who would have such services at the bank of a stream.

It always gave me a keenly bewitching feeling to approach a revival service in the woods at night, with the light from candles or kerosene lamps flickering through doors and windows or trees and with the lusty singing of opening hymns sounding in the air. It took the mind completely away from thoughts about farm drudgery, either of the day or the morrow. The singing generally surpassed the sermon in this emotional fulfillment for most of us. We inevitably observed the disruptions or distractions with which the minister had to compete, such as mothers going outside with crying babies or boys and girls passing in and out and carrying on conversation. A young fellow at my church once walked out in the middle of a sermon, and the squeaking of his new shoes was heard all over the house. Said the preacher, "If there is anybody else with new shoes to show, let him go now." One night, just as the preacher was using the words, "There it goes," and pointing an arm outward, an embarrassed woman, with a baby in arms, stumbled and fell out of the door, ruining his point, or making it.

The rural revival has furnished welcome opportunities for social life. It has been a happy occasion for young men to escort young women to and from church, to sit with them on the women's side of the aisle if the separation of the sexes was not too rigid, or perhaps to sing with them in the choir. An old resident of Rome has described how he and his buddies made church dates with girls in Cherokee County, Alabama, some sixty years ago. In late afternoon, the boy would ride along the road, stop in front of a house where a suitable girl would be sitting on the front porch dressed for church, and ask, "You got company for church tonight?" If the girl was available and he was acceptable, she answered, "No," and he dismounted to become the "company." If he was not acceptable, the answer was "Yes," whether true or false, and he kept moving, hoping for better luck at the next stop.

Boys and girls have often come to evening services separately and left church together, rivals sometimes scrambling to get to a popular girl first. I once saw two fellows thus get into each other's way and resort to shoving as one got on the other's toes in beating him to the girl. Boys without girls to escort have been known to play tricks on the more fortunate, such as chasing a fellow and throwing rocks at him as he returned from the girl's house after seeing her home, unless he changed his course and made a good dodge. This exceptional treatment might be more likely administered to a youngster from outside the community paying attention to one of "our girls."

The extensive use of revival preaching and singing has been an important factor in the popularity of Methodist and Baptist denominations in the hill country from the days of the first settlers to the era of Sam Jones and after. These groups numerically lead all others in this region, with Presbyterians in third place and others bringing up the rear. They lead among white and colored, ranking next to the "big church" of non-members. I once heard a Negro preacher make the comment, "As the white folks say, when Negroes ain't Methodists or Baptists, somebody's been tampering with 'em."

Revivals are still conspicuous among churches of these Protestant denominations. But the meetings have less fervor and shouting than they once had, and they have less community significance. The old-time religious fervor has passed over to various Holiness or "Holy Roller" and Church of God groups, which are raking in members in mill villages and rural hamlets and invading urban centers. The old Asbury Methodist church of my boyhood has disappeared, and a larger "Holy Roller" center has sprung up nearby. Negro Methodists and Baptists do not shout like they used to, but they have not yielded ground to the Holiness cults as have the whites. There is evidently little likelihood that Negroes will join those rural mountaineers who handle rattlesnakes in their religious worship. Only whites have been jailed for that type of "disorderly conduct," as at Chattanooga in the autumn of 1945.

The Primitive, or "Hardshell," Baptists, with their ancient rite of footwashing, have constituted a minor denomination in the rural hills. They have been important in certain isolated communities, though sons and daughters have been departing from the faith upon wider contact with the world. Their isolation has, in a sense, been spiritual as well as physical, for their religious belief and practice exclude missionary enterprise. Many "Hardshell" members have been good farmers on their own lands, with more production for home consumption than for the market. With limited book learning, they have been good neighbors among themselves. I know that they have brought full baskets, for dinner on the ground, to the annual footwashing, an all-day service, with numerous preachers taking the pulpit in turn.

I have attended their all-day meetings in spring and observed the uneducated ministers in action, each seemingly trying to surpass the others in loudness of voice in his singsong peroration. They said much about salvation and religious experience but avoided the Sam Jones type of temperance argument. The crowd was several times too large for the meeting house, but the sound of preaching could be heard by all. Only a small proportion of the multitude were

"Hardshells." The occasion was an outing for many, including visitors from two or three towns. "City slickers" went home making funny comments about the plain food and "soggy biscuits," though they had eaten heartily when dinner was spread. The members' serious ceremony of washing each other's feet in the afternoon was a highlight for many spectators, with an occasional observation that all feet seemed unusually clean before the washing began.

The rural hill country has been fed Protestant orthodoxy more exclusively than any other part of America. It has had a minimum exposure to Episcopalian and Roman Catholic influences, being different in this respect from people in other regions of the South. It has had no contact with Unitarianism. It has had doctrinal controversies, as between Methodists and Baptists or between Baptists and Baptists. There have been disputes over methods of baptism, infant baptism, free will, predestination, and whether women should speak in church. The disputes have sometimes spread to argumentative laymen. Discussion of these issues has added dullness to many a sermon, with most members uninterested in such matters. Not doctrines but other factors have often determined membership, as in the case of a hillbilly who could not tell whether it was a Methodist, Baptist, or Presbyterian church that he belonged to. All this fellow knew was that he had gone to the mourners' bench and joined at Bethel. Conflicting doctrines have had followers in the same family without causing friction. A popular politician of North Alabama made the chivalrous comment that his wife, a Methodist, believed in falling from grace but never fell, while, as a Baptist, he believed that there was no fall, but fell every day.

The rural and small-town orthodoxy has tended to neglect or oppose scientific thought as it affects the fundamentalist acceptance of the Bible as literally true "from cover to cover, with every comma." In the school of my first teaching experience, local ministers complained to the president because a devout teacher of science was spreading modernistic religious views among the students. Circuit riders have disposed of ideas of evolution by referring to Sam Jones as saying that, in too many cases, the theory works backward, with men making monkeys of themselves.

Aside from the anti-liquor crusade, these orthodox ministers have, with striking exceptions, viewed the social scene with relative unconcern. Personal soul-salvation for the other world takes precedence over working for community salvation and social justice in this one. A Southern Baptist minister, Edwin McNeill Poteat, Jr., confirmed this estimate of his Protestant colleagues a few years ago in his contribution to *Culture in the South.* He might revise his analysis, if rewriting it today, but not sweepingly. He might point to a few preachers between Birmingham and Atlanta who have run into trouble for taking cognizance of social problems and labor relations. But he could point to plenty who are fenced in by the *status quo.*

The ministers of the hills have been deeply concerned with the spiritual life of individuals. Many can claim credit not only for saving sinners "from the wrath to come," but also for aiding and inspiring them to useful careers. Without the techniques of modern psychology, they have done yeomen service in the field of personality adjustment. They have comforted persons of illegitimate offspring and enabled them to overcome the stigma of being "woods colts." In getting next to such a fellow and making him active in church work, a small-town preacher said, "He is more dependent on the church than anybody else." That process has led to outstanding civic leadership. Through personal contact, circuit riders and local preachers have planted ideals in minds of the young and caused them to hunger for more education, perhaps through a church school. They have influenced them to move up the ladder of achievement and out of their rural community. They missed ministering to the majority, but they moved into old age with consoling feelings of having influenced a worthy minority along the way.

Many of these rural ministers have made good as fathers and disapproved the popular notion that preachers' sons turn out badly. William Homer Spencer, a distinguished dean of the University of Chicago, and Robert Lester, secretary of the richly endowed Carnegie Corporation, were born at unincorporated places in the Coosa Valley, the sons of circuit riders. So was Bishop Hoyt M. Dobbs, of the Methodist Church. F. T. J. Brandon, who spent decades preaching over North Alabama before and after 1900, raised up one son to become a successful minister and another to become a genial politician and governor. Negro ministers of the countryside have been successful in influencing home and family.

Many who caught a spirit of personal religion and progress through the rural church and its ministry moved on to town or city to seek success in business or industry. It was a case of Protestant individualism and economic laissez-faire combining under the same clear conscience. It was good stewardship, which brought praise from the preacher, who often pointed to the practice of religion as favorable to success in business. Country women, moving to town, have taken their religion with them and made their social adjustments through the church.

The itinerant ministers of the countryside have spent most of their time on the road or in private homes, where much of their influence has been felt. At rural revivals, the visiting ministers, especially in horse-and-buggy days, would rotate from home to home for meals and lodging and prayer with the family. As a child I was always glad for them to come to our house, for their visit generally meant chicken for dinner and ham for breakfast, with various other good things to eat. They often brought interesting comments. One presiding elder kept us waiting an ungodly long time for the children's "second table," for he got started at dinner on the story of his seven-year courtship, in which he was successful in winning both a wife and the final consent of her financially successful father, whose religious convictions stopped short of wanting a poor preacher for son-in-law.

Human material to link old religion and new progress was found in the career of Henry Grady, who was a friend of many ministers, including Sam Jones. An impressive story, perhaps embellished in the retelling, was an account of the journalist's going back to the home of his "old mother" in North Georgia, confessing to her that he had been doing wrong, and asking her to treat him as a child again for purposes of prayer. Her chair became a mourner's bench, the son repented of sins, the mother prayed for forgiveness, and there was a spiritual renewal. Revival leaders brought tears from audiences with this story of "that great editor," who incidentally called upon his mother also for more worldly aid to meet financial reverses. Grady believed in religion and also tried his luck in dealing in cotton "futures."

7

Songs of the Hills

ALL-DAY SINGING and dinner on the ground and folks a-coming from fifteen miles around. Leaders with tuning forks singing anything in sight. Do, re, mi, and everybody sings, first the notes and then the words. Singing with inspiration and perspiration. Leaders take turn in leading, each does his best, and they call each other brother. Meeting in a church or meeting in a courthouse and opening with prayer. Sermons in tunes for two or three hours in the morning and longer in the afternoon. Many come to sing. Some come not to sing, but to stay outside and visit. "Where's that feller going in that borrowed buggy?" "To the singing and he's going to haul some calico." "Grandma, let's go to the all-day singing and dinner on the ground." "No, child, no, whiskey in the bushes and the devil all around."

The hill country has been a land of singing. It has not equaled the lowlands in Negro spirituals and plantation melodies. It has not equaled the earlier Appalachian settlements in preserving old English ballads. But it has given lusty emphasis to Old Baptist hymns, *Sacred Harp* numbers, and newer gospel songs. Annual singing conventions are held in cities of this region, thousands attending the Guntersville session on a Sunday in May. They sing "white spirituals" from the *Sacred Harp*, a book which was first published at Philadelphia in 1844 "for the proprietors, B. F. White and E. J. King" of Hamilton on Georgia's western border. Since 1890 great quantities of non-denominational song books in paper covers at low prices have been published at the old hill town of Dalton, Georgia, by the A. J. Showalter Company, under such titles as *Gospel Songs, New Harmony,* and *The Highway to Heaven*. Rural churches and singing groups have acquired stacks of Showalter books, which have also gone into private homes along with catalogues of mail-order houses. Wide use has worn out many a copy.

These books have been in demand at camp meetings and other revivals. The singing of "The Old Time Religion" has made many people shout, especially after an eloquent sermon. When preachers at night vividly depicted immediate dangers of hell-fire, citing examples of sinners who suddenly died while considering repentance, and urged the unsaved to hesitate no longer, stirring feelings have been produced by a mass singing of "Almost Persuaded." There was inner weeping, if not external tears, for the fate of those who refused to come to the mourners' bench as the song progressed to the words, "almost, but lost."

Much of this folk singing has been without aid of organ or piano or separate choir. It has seldom yielded to solos or solo parts. As a country boy I was over fifteen years old and had been to town several times before I knew there was such a practice as giving a solo before an audience. Several of the favorite hymns, like "The Old Time Religion" and "Over Yonder," repeat lines and words, besides the chorus, so that they can be sung without the book after the leader or preacher "histes the tune." This has been helpful when there were too few books, poor lighting at night, and participants who could not read. "Lining the hymn" was a lingering custom in the backwoods. In this practice, the preacher would read out the words, a line or two at the time, with the audience repeating the words responsively in song. Under the promptings of the spirit, he might adopt a sort of chant. A story handed down through my mother alleges that one night the preacher, unable to read further on account of a poor light, wished his worshipers to continue on their own. Without change of tone or manner, he said, "Sing," and added the words, "My eyes are dim; I can not see," which the congregation took up and sang to the tune of "Amazing Grace," pausing for another line. If this story stemmed from the incident which Jean Thomas relates in amplified form as "tradition" in *Blue Ridge Country*, it came a few hundred miles by word of mouth and changed its setting from Kentucky to Alabama.

These old tunes and titles have been dear to the memory of many up-country people, including Negroes. They furnished material to Frank L. Stanton for poetic comment in his "Songs of the Soil," which appeared for years as a column in the Atlanta *Constitution*. The titles have been used for pointed description, as when a farmer with large feet got a new pair of heavy shoes and was told to sing "How Firm a Foundation." A Negro worker, devoted to his church and his union said he would be CIO, "When the roll is called up yonder."

The body of religious folk song, so important in the up-country, had earlier beginnings elsewhere, and its influence has spread beyond the hills. Singers along the way have made modifications and additions, and Negro spirituals represent still other adaptations in words and tunes.

The Georgians' *Sacred Harp* collection announced "nearly one hundred pieces never before published." It was preceded by *Southern Harmony*, which was first published in 1835 at New Haven, Connecticut, for "Singin' Billy" Walker, of Spartanburg, South Carolina, who boasted of "nearly one hundred new tunes, which have never before been published." This book, with its shaped notes for easy reading, was sold in general stores of the rural South along with groceries and tobacco, reaching a circulation of 600,-000 copies by 1860. It was used by Walker in hundreds of singing schools which he taught in the Carolinas, East Tennessee, and Georgia. After the first publication he always signed his name, "William Walker, A.S.H.," the title signifying "Author of Southern Harmony." Part of the inscription on his Spartanburg gravestone reads: "A consistent Baptist 47 yrs. Taught music 45 yrs. The Author of 4 Books of sacred music." It was said that he died with melodies on his tongue. His *Southern Harmony* was reproduced with introductory information by the Federal Writers' Project of Kentucky in 1939, for this upland singer had a wide following in the Bluegrass state.

The Southern publications and singing practices followed the New England patterns, which came down from colonial times, largely through the pioneer Baptists. George Pullen Jackson, in his *White Spirituals of the Southern Uplands*, says that the shape-note singing movement spread from New England through Pennsylvania to the South and West, with the Yankee singing master carrying the rural music methods into the newer regions. He lists thirty-eight song books in the four-shape notation, with publication dates ranging from 1798 to 1855 and with sponsors or authors spread from Connecticut to Georgia and Missouri.

Jackson shows that many tunes of these folk hymns were borrowed from secular folk songs and ballads. In *The Story of the Sacred Harp* he notes that *"Wondrous Love"* has a tune and a stanza form which were taken "From the worldly song about the famous pirate, Captain Kidd." In his estimate of the simple words and tunes of this class of song, he expresses the conviction that *"Sacred Harp* music must be sung and not heard."

In recent years a gospel-song publishing industry of mass-production proportions has sprung up in the hill country. It has employed a high-pressure salesmanship, and the quality of the musical product is questionable, as Jackson and others point out. Many songs brought out since 1940 by publishers at Chattanooga, Dalton, and elsewhere are distinctly prosaic and second-rate. Such new songs as "Step over the Line," "Pray on," and "Hand in Hand with Jesus" cannot compare with the old-time favorites. There are striking parallels between certain of the white and Negro spirituals of the South, but few of the newer productions will become two-race spirituals. The publishers, however, take care to mix old and new songs in the books they put out in great numbers for profit. And *Sacred Harp* singings continue to attract the faithful for distances even of hundreds of miles.

The hill people have secular songs and ditties, songs from the mountains, songs from the plains, and snatches right out of the hills. There has been wide use of fiddle tunes for square dances, like "Turkey in the Straw." I used to hear "Shortenin' Bread" sung and played on a harmonica or "French harp," and sometimes on a jew's-harp, often for clog-dancing. I remember a song for a kissing game, which is popular in Mississippi. Boys and girls form a ring, hold hands, and march around a person in the center. They start singing,

> *We're marching round the levee,*
> *We're marching round the levee,*
> *We're marching round the levee,*
> *For we have gained the day.*

Other stanzas are based on such lines as, "Go forth and choose your lover." "I kneel because I love you," "I measure my love to show you," and finally, "I'll take a kiss and leave you."

Other songs for kissing games in my experience are "Johnny Brown" and "Under the Juniper Tree." The latter opens up with

> *Old Brother Silas, how merry was he,*
> *The night he sat under the juniper tree,*
> *The juniper tree, hi O, hi O, hi O,*
> *The juniper tree, hi O.*

For a girl as "victim" it would be,

> *Old Sister Phoebe, how merry was she....*

The last stanza has the line,

> *Take a sweet kiss, it will do you no harm.*

Fireside favorite in the rural hills has been "Billy Boy."
Two stanzas, as I have heard them, run,

> *O where are you going, Billy Boy, Billy Boy?*
> *O where are you going, charming Billy?*
>
> *O I'm going to seek a wife,*
> *She's the joy of my life;*
> *She's a young thing and can not leave her mother.*
>
> *Can she bake a cherry pie, Billy Boy, Billy Boy?*
> *Can she bake a cherry pie, charming Billy?*
>
> *She can bake a cherry pie*
> *As quick as a cat can bat an eye;*
> *She's a young thing and can not leave her mother.*

Mothers have mournfully hummed babies to sleep with
this version of "The Old Gray Goose":

> *Go tell Aunt Tabby,*
> *Go tell Aunt Tabby,*
> *Go tell Aunt Tabby,*
> *Her old gray goose is dead.*

Songs of the Hills

The one she's been saving,
The one she's been saving,
The one she's been saving,
To make a featherbed.

I first learned about Jesse James from a Negro farm worker, who told the story many times, always turning to song and ending with the line,

They laid poor Jesse in his grave.

Many are the two-line and four-line pieces which have served for work songs on farm and road and construction jobs. Often I have heard Negroes sing,

Chickens on my back
Hounds on my track,
Go'in' to make it to my shanty way back.

Workers often sing of women. I have heard several variations of "Ida Red," and also such jingles as,

O my honey, I'm tired of you,
Not only you, but the way you do.

O honey, when I had you
The di'monds you wo'!
Now some other scutler's got you,
Barefooted you go.

Not only women, but wickedness must be noted in song, and

> *Nobody knows how mean I am*
> *Till I get my whiskey dram.*

As to the officer of the law,

> *O Mr. Johnson, turn me loose;*
> *I got no money but a good excuse.*

Negro workers of the hills sang of meat rationing long before World War II.

> *What you go'n' to do when the meat gives out,*
> > *Baby?*
> *What you go'n' to do when the meat gives out,*
> > *Baby?*
> *What you go'n' to do when the meat gives out?*
> *Sit in the corner with a lip poked out,*
> > *Baby.*
> *What you go'n' to do when the meat comes in,*
> > *Baby?*
> *What you go'n' to do when the meat comes in,*
> > *Baby?*
> *What you go'n' to do when the meat comes in?*
> *Sit in the corner with a greasy chin,*
> > *Baby.*

Foremen, "straw bosses," and work leaders have improvised chants to synchronize the labor of gangs loading, unloading, and placing heavy steel and timber for railroad work, bridge building, and the like. This was especially true before mechanical power replaced human "elbow grease" for handling materials. There is an Alabama hill-country version of "John Henry," which sadly emphasizes the theme of the passing of the human steel driver and the coming of the power-driven drill. I have heard many chants that are similar to the steel-laying yell which John and Alan Lomax recorded from the lips of Rochelle Harris, of Chattanooga, and reproduced in their *American Ballads and Folk Songs*.

I have a mental sound picture of Ed Newsome, a "steel driver," and his partner, who was "shaking steel" for him as Ed hammered away to send the drill into the lime rock for a dynamite blast. The shaking comes between hammerings, and the hammer must not miss the top of the drill if the shaker's hands are to escape smashing. Ed chants, over and over and over, the two words, "I belong," as he lifts and readies the hammer on his shoulder, each chant ending with the downward stroke of the hammer on the drill. After an interval, Ed pauses briefly, giving warning with a complete sentence,

I belong to the steel driving crew.

wildlife of the region enters into such farm songs as,

> *Possum up the simmon tree,*
> *Raccoon on the ground;*
> *Raccoon to the possum say,*
> *Shake them simmons down.*

or

> 'As I was going cross the fiel'
> 'A black-snake bit me on the heel;
> I jumped the fence 'cause I thought it was best,
> I jumped smack in a hornets' nest.

Negro spirituals serve to lighten wash-day duties. I have heard women cotton-choppers sing,

> I am climbing Jacob's ladder,
> Don't you grieve after me.

A companion piece is,

> If that preacher asks for me,
> Tell him I'm gone to Galilee;
> I ought'o been there ten thousand years,
> Drinking wine,
> Drinking wine, wine, wine,
> Drinking wine, wine, wine;
> I ought'o been there ten thousand years,
> Drinking wine.

The most stirring secular song in my region for years was "Dixie." The coming of Northern industries and Northern business leaders did not moderate enthusiasm for this song as long as there were good numbers of Confederate veterans like John Patterson to shout when it was played or sung. John lived in the Coosa Valley, not far from Gadsden, and regularly read the weekly edition of Henry Grady's *Constitution*. He apologized for going wild at a sober school gathering, but the song made him cut loose as if he had "got religion" at a camp meeting. "Dixie" connected the Old and New South.

8

Rustic Wit and Laughing Stock

―――――――

BUD MEDDERS, lean and tall share-tenant, was feeling good under the influence of two drinks of corn liquor. He was entertaining the loafers at our country store, loafers waiting for the evening train to pass and leave the mail. Looking down at his well-behaved dog at his feet, he began to praise him, and led up to the statement:

"That dog will do anything in the world that I want him to."

"Tell him," urged a bystander, "to go under the table there and lie down."

Immediately, but deliberately, Bud declared, "I don't want him to do that."

As one of the loafers started out the door, Bud asked, "Where are you going, John?"

John replied, "I don't know Bud, I may just go straight up."

"You'll have to cut your feet off first," observed Bud, as he continued with other topics.

Rustic Wit and Laughing Stock

As a farmer, Bud had to bend his long frame to help his family with the cotton picking in the autumn. He said that the sight of the first open boll in August gave him the backache. He once went to town to get an aching tooth pulled. But the ache ceased as he reached the dentist's door, and he backed out. On the next occasion, he bought a nickel's worth of stick candy and chewed on it all the way to the dental chair. When two or three attempts failed to bring forth the tooth, Bud said to the man at the job, "Wait a minute. I want to ask you a question. Can you tell me where I can find a dentist?"

He sent word one day by a group of boys to the district school teacher that he was starting to school as soon as he could get a last year's almanac to study, the teacher having become exasperated at the variety of texts brought in and sarcastically remarked that he was ready to have almanacs added to the collection.

At the time of the Spanish-American War, Bud got a rumor that there would be conscription, and he also heard that a Spanish immigrant was working over in the "coaling," where wood was turned into charcoal. So he wanted the postmaster to write to Washington to get permission for him to kill the local Spaniard as his part in winning the war. Later he went home and tested his wife's affection by giving a glowing report about the imminence of conscription and seeing her go into tears until his snickering relieved her tension.

Everybody laughed with Bud or at him, whether he was sober or was drunk enough to boast like a Paul Bunyan and to want to eat alive some fellow who was not present. At the drunkest, he was "free-born, white, and twenty-one" and didn't "give a goddam." His comical ways and words appealed to countrymen and townsmen alike. As worker or loafer, he broke the monotony of life on the countryside.

Bud Medders, as a natural-born humorist of the hills, was an unheralded descendant of Bill Arp, whom Charles H. Smith captured and paraded across the pages of books and newspapers. Smith, who came to be widely known as Bill Arp, was a contemporary of Henry Grady and Sam Jones and hailed from their section of North Georgia. Like the other two, he looked at the New South in the making and found something to say. He extracted matter for humorous comment from the juxtaposition of town and country, of industrialism and provincial ruralism. He brought the countryman to town and exposed him very much after the manner in which A. B. Longstreet, of the Old South, had exposed the frontier rube to sophisticated planter society in *Georgia Scenes*. He had another forerunner in Johnson J. Hooper, antebellum newspaper man of the hill town of Dadeville, Alabama, and other points, who created or discovered Simon Suggs and wrote backwoods sketches that delighted educated lowlanders. But, more than Hooper and Longstreet, he gave a penetrating discussion of the affairs of the day under his hillbilly mask.

For years I read Bill Arp articles or letters in the Atlanta *Constitution* without realizing that Smith was the real name of the humorous commentator who displayed the horse sense of a good countryman. I was set straight by the news of his death and contact with his books, one of them entitled *From the Uncivil War to Date, 1861-1903*.

Charles H. Smith was a young lawyer of Rome in the

eighteen fifties. He wrote an open letter to "Abe Linkhorn" in 1861, and, for purposes of anonymity, he signed it "Bill Arp," with the consent of the Georgia "Cracker" of that name, for Bill asserted that "them's my sentiments." Thus "Bill Arp" became the symbol for a political writer and cracker-box philosopher, serving the function of identification instead of anonymity. Smith, in using that pen-name, undertook to idealize "the language and humor of an unlettered countryman," and the result was a mixture of Arp and himself, with a bond of sympathy between author and character.

The real Bill Arp, according to the writer who appropriated his name, was a small, tough, and active fellow, who "could out-run, out-jump, out-swim, out-wrestle, out-shoot anybody" who starred at gander-pullings, but who left most of the home chores to his wife and children. His wife had to come for him and take him home in frequent instances of drunkenness. Private Arp became a prankster and campfire favorite in the Civil War. He said he killed as many of the Yankees as they did of him.

Through the processes of time and evolution, Smith's Bill Arp was less crude and more respectable than Longstreet's Ned Brace, and Bud Medders was an improvement on both without any literary build-up. Bud could go off with gun and dog and bring in squirrels and rabbits. He was not afraid of work, though he did not love it. He was a good farmer and even kept his wife supplied with stove-wood. If he sometimes got drunk when he sold cotton, he went home on his own power and with most of the money he had received after paying his debts. When he changed landlords and moved, it was through his own choice and restlessness. He became sufficiently modern to neglect or abandon the Hardshell Baptist faith of his fathers. In politics he did not always know what candidates to support, but he emphasized that he knew whom to vote against, for he wanted to turn or keep the rascals out. In that light he "seed" his civic duty and "done it."

Bud and his kind have had leading roles, not only in country store sessions, but in various gatherings, including sorghum-mill groups at night. Grinding sorghum for the juice and cooking the juice into syrup with portable equipment have furnished an institutional feature of autumn activity in the hills. Sorghum syrup, with its good vitamin content, must be associated with the Southern Piedmont as distinctively as maple syrup and sugar with New England. It has been an important item for rural candy pullings and a redeeming factor in the diet of hillbillies. I once knew of a family that kept a five-gallon lard can of sorghum on the dining table all the time for steady self-service. By the proper recipe, it gives character, color, and sweetness to cake with no dependence on commercial sugar. It has served in the making of wildcat liquor.

Sorghum is holding its own as a farm product. But the coming into use of the large stationary establishment, with mechanical power and scientific methods of processing is putting an end to the picturesque little mill and its accompanying type of stag party. Bud Medders could criticize the TVA for furnishing power and other technical encouragement to bring about this change. However, he would not object to the quality of the modern product, for it tastes like the best of the old days.

The old-time sorghum makers move from stand to stand

with two two-horse wagons, one wagon carrying the mill and the other the pan. At each stand the stripped and harvested cane from the crops of two or three or more neighbors is assembled. The spot is very likely in or near a sorghum field. For the best results in quantity and quality, it is important to make the sorghum without delay after the cane is cut. So operation goes on steadily day and night until all the cane at one place is made up. The farmer whose cane is being processed must furnish wood for heating the pan, labor to feed cane to the mill, and perhaps mules to pull the lever in a merry-go-round fashion to operate the mill with its revolving rollers, which press the juice from the cane. He must also provide meals for the sorghum makers, who want snacks and coffee at midnight. He must bring containers for his sorghum.

With a mule or two a-tramping round and round, cane a-cracking, and syrup a-cookin, there is always something doing at the sorghum mill. There are calls for more wood for the fire, more cane for the mill, more juice for the pan. There is a continual dipping or scraping of the greenish "skimmings" from the cooking mixture, with a small hole in the ground to receive this thick and messy liquid. It is sometimes a prank to maneuver a straggler into stepping or stumbling into the "skimming hole," even by concealing it temporarily with a light covering.

Night comes, and more people gather. A syrupy odor fills the air. Light from pine-knots burning on an elevated platform gives a campfire effect to the scene. Farm dogs howl or hang around the place. Men like Bud Medders crack jokes, tell stories, and review all the recent devilment of the community. I once saw them gang up and torment a fellow who could not take a joke, until a man said, "Let that boy alone. He had typhoid fever, and it ruined his mind."

The sorghum mill crowd at Possum Trot built up a story one night about a white sharecropper, which brought a hearty response from the Negroes and illustrated the psychological meaning of the saying, "I'd ruther be a nigger than a po' white man." The story concerned a fellow called Mack, who lived behind a big wooded hill from his boss, another tenant representing the landlord, who was living in Florida. The absent Mack seemed to have no friend in the party, and there was no bar to comments. He had made a poor crop, poorer than was once made on the same land by Walt Campbell, a Negro who was present with a load of cane to make up. His corn crop was especially short. Some of the corn had disappeared from the field before time for gathering it and dividing it. The boss had found tracks, blurred by rain, in rows where corn was missing. They said that Mack said, "The tracks must 'a' been bear tracks."

Walt Campbell led the laughter.

The sorghum maker observed that it was "a two-legged bear," and Walt roared.

"Mack made them tracks," said another, "and he was the bear that got that corn."

All let loose, and Walt rolled on the ground with jerks of laughter. When he quieted down, another colored man repeated the last "bear" comment, and Walt roared and rolled again, supplanting Mack as a cause of laughter for the group. It took him several minutes to recover to the stage of a moderate chuckle, and then he said in broken words, "The first time I heard that joke—I heard it last week—it nearly killed me."

There is no white supremacy in wit and humor, and Negroes of the hills have indulged their fancy in this field with a less conspicuous subserviency than is characteristic of colored people in the plantation country. Luke Hudson, forty years a good sharecropper on the same upland farm, could give pretty sane advice. He told a youngster, who was later a lawyer, to "trust no living person and walk carefully among the dead." A well-to-do ex-slave in my community said the Civil War interfered with his plan to buy his own freedom and purchase a slave to work for him. The most apt and artistic mimic I ever knew was "Cleve," a mulatto. He could reproduce the words and ways of any person, man or woman, black or white, to the delight of any group. He was especially good at "taking off" a gossipy and philosophical white woman, who got a son-in-law through a "shotgun wedding" and who said, "What I am I am, and nobody can't make me no ammer."

Much of the witty and humorous comment by white and colored hillbillies is appropriated and adapted from other sources and used for original purposes. Charley Maner, a railroad section worker, used to attribute sayings of Benjamin Franklin to Uncle Robert McCain, from whom he had first heard them. Jeff Harbin, a fiddler for square dances, who came from Cherokee County, Alabama, and settled in Calhoun, read the Chicago *Saturday Blade* and other papers and then retailed the odd comments, often attributing them to Cherokee County. A lie detector applied to him would hardly have separated Cherokee fact from Cherokee fiction, so thoroughly were they intermingled in his mind. After he became a justice of the peace he developed a repertoire of unique courthouse stories, glowingly associating most of these with his native county, which incidentally did not contain an incorporated town. He enjoyed telling how rural witnesses put it over high-class lawyers, as in the case of a stolen and slaughtered calf, with the recovered hide serving as identifying evidence. When the cross-examining attorney asked the country boy where he first saw that hide, the youngster snapped out the answer, "On the calf, of course." The lawyer, in Jeff Harbin language, was "like the little boy the calf ran over; he didn't have anything to say."

The hill people have feasted on stories and sayings by or about Davey Crockett, Bob Taylor, Tennessee's fiddling governor, Bill Arp, Sam Jones, and Bill Brandon, the North Alabama preacher's son, fox-and-possum hunter, and governor of Alabama. Bill could regale voters with hunting stories, including incidents of his boyhood. Once he came home from a night hunt when he should have gone to the revival meeting his daddy was conducting. As he stumbled over a chair in the dark and waked up his father, he saved himself from a whipping by speaking out in Scriptural language, "Foxes have holes and birds of the air have nests, but the son of Brandon hath not where to lay his head." Once in a campaign he was about to lose votes on account of his silk socks, for which a rival denounced him. But he saved the day and confounded his critic by appearing suddenly before an audience and conspicuously lifting his trousers to show bare legs at his shoe tops.

Hillbillies picked up tall tales from the Paul Bunyan

series. My introduction to these stories was at country school on the Friday afternoon occasions when every pupil was supposed to recite a chosen piece. The larger boys, considering themselves above rendering bits of poetry, made hits sometimes with Bunyan material. A couple of Hardshell Baptists were best at this. They mastered their subject and seemed to take on Bunyan roles.

The Slow Traveler Through Arkansas in its day furnished subject matter for barnyard gossip at noontime and on rainy days. It was sometimes purchased from newsboys on trains. Abridged versions of the more folksy "Arkansas Traveler" have also spread through the up-country.

In the realm of feminine humor, Grady's *Constitution* featured a weekly column by Mrs. E. B. Ploughman, who wrote in the style of a hillbilly woman under the name of "Betsy Hamilton." Rural women of the hills loaned and borrowed cheap copies of *Samantha at Saratoga; or "Flirtin' with Fashion,"* by "Josiah Allen's Wife," a book brought out in 1887 by Marietta Holley, of rural New York. To their own region they applied much of the contents, language, and spelling of this work, such as this description of a striking character:

"Her dress wuz a stiff, sort of shinin' poplin, made tight acrost the chest and elboes. And her hat had some stiff feathers in it that stood up straight and sort a sharp lookin'. She had a long sharp breast-pin sort of stabbed in through the front of her stiff standin' collar, and her knuckles sot out through her firm lisle thread gloves, her umbrella wuz long and wound up hard to that extent I have never seen before nor sense. She wuz, take it all in all, a hard sight, and skairful."

Women and their menfolk read *Samantha at Saratoga* aloud and chuckled over it without worrying too much about its social meanings. They enjoyed the contrast or clash between the naive and high society, feeling superior to the former and free from the sins of the latter. It was partly for the same double feeling of innocence that they relished the steady stream of witty stories and comment which flowed through the sermons of Sam Jones and later preachers like George R. Stuart, who invariably attracted hundreds of visitors to his Methodist services in Birmingham.

Much of this wit and humor is inherently as "old as the hills," but it takes on originality and effectiveness in the telling. It is better spoken than written. It is enhanced by the oral narrative power, personality, and background reputation of the performer. For a striking example of this I might cite Andrew Lytle's account of the weaning of "Brother Micajah," a story known in the hills and elsewhere. Lytle, who is a product of Middle Tennessee and North Alabama, is incidentally a collector, writer, and speaker of tales of the plain people. This particular story concerns the serious matter of weaning a stubborn "youngun," who has fed too long at his mother's breast, a practice by no means unknown in the rural hills. Between dips of snuff, the mother and a visiting neighbor discuss the problem, and the neighbor advises that a concoction of lard, quinine, and alum be applied to the breast for the next feeding. The recipe is used, and late in the day the son enters. He leaps with cat-like prowess as he puts his hunting rifle in its place on the wall. Then he announces his hunger, receiving the welcome, "Come and get it." Upon first contact with his meal he jerks his head up and yells, "Pa, give me a chaw of terbacker; ma's been eatin' bitterweed."

This story, with its mixed elements of truth, exaggeration, and surprise, offers rich opportunities for supporting details and facial solemnity. Lytle handles it with understanding humor from the beginning to the side-splitting finish.

There is native wit in "them thar hills," and it can still be discovered by searchers like Andrew Lytle or Ralph McGill, who is on the newspaper of Henry Grady and Bill Arp and, in a way, combines the roles of both. But rural humor is losing its primacy, except as an antique piece, with the coming of industrial days and industrial ways. It is yielding place to the syndicated metropolitan column. Not a new Bill Arp, but a Walter Winchell is read and quoted in the rural South. The present-day country store offers little opportunity or encouragement to a Bud Medders. The dilemma of the countryman who would remain a countryman is summed up in the words, "I just sets on the porch and thinks, and sometimes I just sets."

The rural folk humor of the hill country came up against an arrested development virtually at its beginning. In most of this section only half a generation intervened between the removal of the Indians and the rise of a strong industrial consciousness, with an emphasis on outside capital and a new outlook. The pre-industrial lore is limited, and the region has appealed more to "Pig Iron" Kelley and the *Manufacturer's Record* than to literary observers. Writers dealing with human items tend to pass by except for brief stops at Birmingham, Atlanta, and Chattanooga. They show greater interest in the more mountainous country or in the lower and older plantation country. So did Jonathan Daniels, for instance, in *A Southerner Discovers the South.* So did Carl Carmer in *Stars Fell on Alabama.* With correctness this lively book, with its mixture of folklore and fun-poking, might have borne such an old fashioned title as *A Journey through South Alabama with a Trip from Birmingham to Sand Mountain by a New Yorker Guided by a Son of the Hills Who Avoided His Own Country.* External and internal neglect makes short and simple the human annals of the hills.

9

Ol' Corn Liquor

I got drunk and fell against the wall;
Ol' corn liquor was the cause of it all.

LIZA COBB, a well-built Negro woman, was more than half drunk when she came into our country store on a night before Christmas. I took boyish delight in selling her a couple of Roman candles and handing her matches to light them. It gave me a thrill to see her out in front turning and shooting the candles in all directions, while bystanders, white and colored, dodged and laughed and egged her on.

Home teachings and insistence on temperance could not prevent me from getting a "kick" out of the doings of drunken customers. I enjoyed the liquor-loosened tongue of harmless Wild Bill, who justified his language by observing that "the Bible says 'damn' and there's mill dams." Whiskey clearly has added to the variety, gaiety, and sadness of life in the hills. In giving accounts of happenings which I have personally observed, I must conceal a few real names for the sake of families of the characters and to save myself from trouble as I move about my hill country.

Legal and illegal whiskey is consumed in the hills. The consumers extend from lowly sharecroppers to capitalists and country gentlemen like the one in the Atlanta district who said he was going to stay drunk until Franklin D. Roosevelt left the White House, and eventually had to go away for treatment. Before there were restrictions on routine shipment across state lines, I used to fill out postal-money orders and fix up registered letters for countrymen who were "sending off" for quarts and gallons. A postal clerk at Jacksonville, Alabama, filling out a money-order form for a fellow who could not write, asked the applicant what amount to state on the blank. The man said, "Three gallons."

Besides saloons in the cities and several of the towns, there were wildcat stills and "blind tiger" peddlers in this region when the Reverend Sam P. Jones was denouncing the liquor traffic all over the land. The wooded country between Piedmont, Alabama, and Cedartown, Georgia, was one of the sections where many natives have derived income from turning corn into spirits and selling the product without the benefit of a government license. They often made a speedy check-up on strange visitors by efficient underground methods, and killings sometimes occurred. In that area "Bell Tree" Smith operated for years. "My granddaddy made liquor, my uncle made it, and my people are still making it," said a man who has migrated from those woods to a metropolitan center. In the prohibition era they enjoyed a sort of protective tariff that gave them a market monopoly. But the law occasionally caught up with them, and they took their medicine. In that period I met a man from those parts on a Seaboard train. He was en route to the Alabama State penitentiary, traveling alone with his own commitment papers, under an improvised honor system, as he said, to "show 'em that I'm a man."

Traditions and evidences of moonshine whiskey bob up in the TVA lake country. On a journey down the Tennessee in 1944, I asked the lock tender at Hale's Bar Dam, below Chattanooga, if there were "any wildcat stills around here." He told of contacts and misunderstandings he had experienced with liquor-makers, who thought his motor boat, with "U.S." on it, was transporting a revenue officer. One mountaineer, happy over discovering that he was not a snooping "revenooer," offered him a big jug of his moonshine merchandise. Another inhabitant, with no spring near his shack, said he just used river water and followed every drink with a "swig of corn liquor," which "kills the bugs." The curtailment of licensed whiskey during World War II stimulated illegal activities in coves where the white corn flows. In Georgia, 1645 moonshine stills were raided in 1945.

The illicit making of liquor in isolated hills has often constituted the only method of condensing corn for transportation to a profitable market over long distances and bad roads. Only the liquid product could bear the transportation cost. The activity has thus furnished a primary occupation for many. It has also furnished a little cash to families otherwise entirely dependent upon subsistence farming. It has served to offset declines in farming on eroded lands. It has provided a beverage for home consumption, for toning up or "roping" coffee on a cold morning.

Wildcat stillers like to operate in low-roof structures beside a stream back in a hollow with abundant brush and briers for camouflage. They want good wood, water, and concealment.

The old-timer's way of making corn liquor is slow and laborious, without the use of yeast or barley malt. He shells his corn and sprouts it by pouring hot water through it for several days, using a container with a vent in the bottom to let the water out. He dries the sprouted corn and grinds it into coarse meal, which is turned into mash by adding boiling water. After the mash stands a few days, the stiller breaks it up and pours water and sugar or a syrup substitute over it. Fermentation takes place in the next few days, and the resulting sour liquid, often called "beer," is ready for distillation. It is then put in a closed boiler, or "still," with a spiral "worm" leading through a constant flow of cold water. Slow boiling over a steady fire sends the alcoholic vapors through the "worm," where they are liquefied. Liquor passing through one time is called "singlings." The careful stiller sends it through again and it comes out "doublings." After being run through a charcoal filter, the product, if made just right and with the proper temperature at all stages, has a good "bead" and is almost colorless. It has a fiery taste and a great power to intoxicate, as indicated by such descriptive terms as "white mule" and "white lightnin'."

Whiskey drinking and whiskey issues have divided Protestant families in the hill country. I have known several pairs of brothers, one in the church and the other out, one ever sober and the other frequently drunk, one for prohibition and the other for the open saloon. Rural Methodists, Baptists, and Presbyterians at times have yielded to temptation, as did one brother who fell from a wagon near our Possum Trot store, skinned his head, and ardently urged all in the store to pray for him. Martin McCain, ex-slave and Methodist preacher of my community, frankly told his bishop that he weakened occasionally and took a drink. Butler Green and other Confederate veterans wanted their daily toddy, with a few repetitions at Christmas time.

Tragedies have resulted from drunken sprees, as in the case of Old George, a well-liked farmer near Piedmont, who was run over by a freight train one night and ground into many pieces. One of his sons, a worker away from home, helped recover the remains without realizing for hours that his father was missing. "Pa's going that way if he don't quit his big drunks," he said. Then he wept and screamed and "took it hard" when his pa was taken to the burial ground. This son became a sober man.

Later there was Sam, a good Negro worker, who would read and even recite local items I sent to the Anniston *Hot Blast*. He got drunk on a weekend, and was killed by a train on a grade at night, and that was another item for me to send to the paper.

Big John, deputy sheriff of the Possum Trot community, seized and sampled a supply of bootleg liquor in the nineteen-twenties. He died immediately, for the bad whiskey had been poisoned seemingly for the purpose of tricking Big John, who was an able officer with a love of drink.

One of my rural humorist friends died of burns received while drunk at home alone. A good washwoman, who laundered my shirts for years, died of exposure on a cold night when she fell in a wet field and was too drunk to go on home alone.

Many men of the hills like their coffee strong enough to "float an iron wedge" and their liquor strong enough to "make a rabbit spit in a bulldog's face." It is no wonder that strong drink is back of much of the personal fighting in this country, which has known fewer standing feuds than the Kentucky mountains and fewer duels than the plantation country. Drinking men of Possum Trot have come home with knife, razor, and pistol wounds, and fellows went to the mines in the days of convict leases for drunken fighting. When John Maxwell was operating his "government still" in our part of the country, many managed to get liquor to drink and to get into devilment. The climax was the fatal shooting of a Maxwell son by a Maxwell son-in-law.

I have witnessed physical friction between white men and Negroes. But all the drinking brawls that have come under my observation have been between white and white or between colored and colored, with no interracial damage involved. I once saw a rural Negro chasing his wife, who had been to town and had had something to drink but was outrunning him and his blows as he hurled at her the charge of being "a white man's whore."

Much of the fighting that is stimulated by whiskey involves only temporary ill will. The disposition of the participants often becomes stormy and calm with variations as sudden changes of the weather in the region. This was clearly illustrated for me by Del and Tip, two young colored workers, who had fought occasionally and once got in a terrific mix-up after opportunity for drinking. They disturbed the peace and both sobered up in jail. My daddy sent me to see Del, who had been working for us and living in a house on our farm. I saw him in jail and put before him the proposal that his fine would be paid and charged against his wages, provided he would stay away from Tip's house and consent to prohibiting Tip's coming to his quarters. He would not accept restrictions on the liberty of association between Tip and himself and remained in jail. They still wanted to get together with more drinking and fighting. Another instance was the sharecropper Tom's wife, who called "the law" to put him in jail for coming home fightin' drunk, and then got busy the next day to get him out.

Corn liquor produces comedy as well as tragedy. There was a noisy carrying-on at a Nixon tenant house one winter evening. Investigation revealed that all occupants were absent, but there were two intoxicated visitors without a host, and Dave, a big fellow, whose wife was home alone, was administering a paddling to Fayette, a little fellow, and loudly demanding, "Why in the hell ain't you at home with your wife?" I well remember John, a farmer, whose sober family made a good crop, while the "ol' man" enjoyed his leisure, his pipe and his bottle. Bounce, a hound dog, was his constant companion, especially on the front porch on the hill on summer nights. Man and dog were frequently left alone to enjoy each other's company and put on a performance for the neighbors. The more John drank, the more he talked to the hound on terms of equality. Once when Bounce responded to the night bark of a distant dog, his drunken master gave the reprimand, "Hush up, Bounce, or before you know it, you'll be in bad company."

Less dominant countrymen find ludicrous ways of concealing their whiskey and their drinking from prohibition wives. They scheme like boys up to mischief. "Let's stop here a minute," says my politician friend as we drive through a wooded spot near his home. "I've got a bottle of liquor hid behind that tree." He treats his friends, and then drives on to the house and to Nellie as if nothing had happened. Nooks and corners of barns also furnish favorite spots for storage and consumption out of sight of the women. It is a game which really does not deceive the women, but it works.

Liquor drinking and accompanying activities are productive of good courtroom shows in the hill country. In years past, a police court in Atlanta, with lively comments from the bench, furnished amusement which attracted visitors as if it were vaudeville. Wanderers into trouble were "taken out of circulation" and fellows yielding to evil were "removed from temptation for thirty days." There were defense workers in World War II who occasionally got into drinking affairs and had to pay fines. They were generally able to pay fines, and there was a shrinkage in the number in local work gangs serving under guards.

"Who Hit Frances?" might be the title of the story brought out by a defense worker's trial which I attended at Anniston, Alabama, near the end of the war. The main feature was a front-porch incident in a mountain-gap community one evening after workers had come in from the day shift and taken a little joy ride. There was a fuss and a free-for-all among half a dozen participants, with dodging and falls from the porch. Frances swore that her arm was "broke" by an axe handle wielded by Joe, the defendant. Joe swore that

Frances' father had the axe handle and struck at him. "I ducked," he said, "and heard Frances groan."

The proportion of whiskey drinkers has hardly decreased in the hill country, where wildcat distilling is still known. However, distinctly fewer men go on long drinking sprees. Less often than formerly does one see a fellow "dead-drunk" or hear of a drunk getting killed by a train or other means. There is generally less liquor hidden about the premises of automobile service stations and public garages than was available in the livery stables of earlier days. It has been many years since a mining engineer of the Birmingham district said a Negro at a dollar a day was the best worker in the world, but a Negro at a dollar and a half a day was the poorest worker in the world, on the assumption that the dollar wage kept him busy, while the higher wage permitted absenteeism and drinking and more absenteeism. It is a declining practice for a Negro to tank up and carry along a razor "for social purposes." There is less fear or feeling that textile mill workers will get drunk and "paint the town red" on Saturday night. It is rarer for farmers to stagger around town squares and country stores on Saturday afternoon.

The rural drinking, such as there is, goes on more openly and perhaps in the home rather than in the barn or behind it. In a sense there is a return of the custom of pioneer days of alcoholic *laissez faire*. On the part of the women there is more likely to be toleration and even participation. There is a decline in the difference in drinking practices between the sexes, between the races, between different parts of town, or between town and country. Fewer brothers are turned out of rural churches for imbibing.

The larger cities of the hill country are very similar to the metropolitan centers of other regions in whiskey doings, whether in store, home, hotel, or club. The town or smaller city is likely to be without legal liquor, partly because of its rural background and partly because there is a majority rural vote in the surrounding county for maintaining prohibition. The resident of a place like Anniston, therefore, may find it necessary or convenient to get his whiskey in Birmingham, Atlanta, or other wet cities, while perhaps griping about the local loss of trade and tax revenue to the less squeamish centers.

The hill country, with many counties more urban than rural by count of towns and noses, has a divided opinion on liquor issues, as on labor and other matters. It takes both its liquor and its religion more moderately than formerly and with less emotional stirrings. It professes a less rigid separation between them, and it takes both with less thought or fear of hellfire and damnation.

10

These Are Our Lives

HARD WORK. Long hours. Low wages. That was the formula of economic development in the up-country in times past and for many years. On that basis did the New South move forward or lag behind the rest of the nation between the end of the Civil War and the beginning of the first World War. Wages and working conditions were better in the industrial Piedmont than in the lowlands. There were fewer cases of peonage or near-peonage in the hills than in the lower country of more planters and more Negro croppers. There were idlers and periods of idleness. But on the whole, the men of the hills were at work, and so were the women. The one-room rural schools functioned in winter and summer, making all children available for farm work in the busy seasons of spring and autumn.

The cotton belt expanded northward and westward. Southern production of the staple trebled in this period, with a crop in 1914 surpassing sixteen million bales. But on a per-capita basis the farm income of the South was just about half of that of the North, and only in the twentieth century did cotton growers enjoy a market that enabled them to lift up their heads and think of much more than the bare necessities of life. By that time the boll weevil had come and serious erosion was at work on the red hills, where soon many millions of farm acres were to be voluntarily abandoned, more than in any other comparable region of the world for such a short period.

Prior to 1900 it was too frequently true that a one-horse farmer produced a cotton crop that sold for less than two hundred dollars, with grain and a few other products for home consumption, but little else for cash. If a cropper, he got only half of this cash; if a share tenant, he got only three-fourths; and, if a landowner, he perhaps had his share cut down by payment on a mortgage debt. In addition there were heavy fertilizer bills to pay, for cotton is a heavy consumer of plant food, besides being a row crop requiring much stirring of the soil and making it easy to wash away. Many were the ills of the "dirt" farmers, who went to bed tired and waked up without hope.

In those hard times a cropper's account or "furnish" to make a crop was sometimes held below fifty dollars, even down to twenty-five. Except for home chickens, vegetables, and a few other items, that account might restrict the diet mainly to side-meat, meal, and molasses. There might be enough flour for occasional use, with fish and game in season. In most instances there was an inclusion of snuff and tobacco, which were sometimes bought in exchange for chickens and eggs. As to the house and household effects, it was said, with a mixture of truth and exaggeration, that such a farmer could study astronomy through the roof and geology through the floor, and that when he moved all he had to do was to call the dog and spit in the fire. There was much moving from farm to farm.

Wage hands on farms in those years worked for seven to ten dollars a month with board. A worker with a family sometimes got thirteen dollars a month and a house to live in. Hoe hands were paid at such rates as forty to sixty cents a day, sometimes "with dinner" at noon. Cotton pickers got thirty-five to forty cents per hundred pounds, a rate which would effectively compete with the mechanical picker today. There was no security of farm wages in the slack seasons of winter and summer.

This scale of wages and income did not provide for much expenditure for clothing by rural people. Those who could afford "Sunday clothes" took special care to make the garments last and last. Not only children but many adults went barefooted when the weather permitted. Shoes worn for Sunday visiting might come back over a shoulder instead of on feet which were unaccustomed to them. Sometimes flour sacks were washed out and ripped open to make women's underwear. Occasionally a farm youngster packed all his belongings in a small flour sack when he went forth to try his luck in the outside world. I have heard old persons in the hills talk about such humble beginnings of successful careers of men of their acquaintance.

Next in importance to the cotton farm was the cotton mill as a source of employment in the hill country. Many families shifted back and forth between cotton tenancy and cotton milling. There were cases of families following both at the same time, with the textile members rising before day on winter mornings by a whistle call and walking from farm to mill in time to start work at six o'clock. The long days of work added up to something like sixty hours a week for a weekly wage that was below ten dollars, far below that sum in the case of young beginners. The wage level was below that paid in New England mills, and it seemed attractive to new capital. It also seemed attractive at the time to most of the farm tenants and mountaineer families who had seen little cash on the farm. But the workers showed a sallow complexion and a tired look, and the girls did not have time to keep particles of lint from their hair. Breakfast and lunch had to be eaten in a hurry.

There were no laws and no unions to interfere with this system of textile labor. Since many of the mills had been set up in a halo of philanthropy as providers of employment, humanitarian movements to regulate them made slow progress. After all, the Southern mill company usually provided houses for working families, houses that were better than most of the farm tenant houses, and, in time, other accommodations such as recreational facilities. It was only natural for individualistic outsiders to let these relations of paternalism and dependency alone. It took years for leaders like Edgar Gardner Murphy, of Alabama, to arouse the public to the importance of putting legislative checks on the abuses of child labor. Additional years, decades, and depressions were to pass before textile workers could bargain collectively and effectively through unions of their own.

Labor conditions and wages in hosiery mills and knitting mills were about the same as in the cotton mills, which were predominantly engaged in making yarn for Eastern factories to process into the finished product. The equipment for knitting and for hosiery and garment manufacture is more easily moved than that of cotton factories, and locations could be changed if labor became unsatisfactory to management. There were fly-by-night "carpetbaggers of industry" in the hill country, looking for cheap labor and local concessions on down to the middle of the nineteen thirties. Thomas L. Stokes, a native Georgian, exposed this racket in a series of Scripps-Howard newspaper articles. He called it a tragic invasion of the South by "makers of shirts, overalls, and other work clothes—some hosiery and shoe factories and an occasional industry of some other type." He found a Tennessee garment plant which had made its fourth move. He found wages as low as four dollars a week and less over prolonged periods for "learners." This was an exploiting of the region's hunger for industry.

Families on eroded hills between Atlanta and Chattanooga developed a unique industry when they undertook to supplement their farm income by making and selling tufted bedspreads. In the period between the two World Wars there was a veritable bedspread boulevard along the route once followed by Sherman's army, with Dalton, Georgia, as its main point. Hughes Reynolds, the Rome writer, calls Dalton "the bedspread capital of the world."

It was by chance a long time ago, says the story, that an Appalachian Mountain woman started the practice of tufting spreads. She was repairing a torn spread, and, lacking thread or yarn, she used a candlewick. Repeating this method, she turned the tufts into a pattern, and then, through suggestions from neighbors, began to dye the wicks. Hence the "candlewick" spreads, with tufts stitched on new ones instead of old ones. Hence such various designs as "Peacock," "Sweet William," "Wedding Ring," and "Barbara Allen."

Yarn, needles, and human fingers combined to produce tufted spreads in the mountain country. The practice and the patterns were taken up by dwellers in the lower Piedmont region, more for profit than for pleasure. Visitors to the hills became interested, and country stores began to handle spreads. The products found a way to markets in the North and East. Middlemen began to buy and sell them, and then to put out the materials and collect the finished work very much in the manner described in George Eliot's *Silas Marner* for handling wool products in pre-industrial England.

This production for cash seemed a godsend for the hill people to whom King Cotton became unkind. It helped when days of depression came along. All members of the family could work at the tufting task, either in spare time or all the time. There were observers who said it was fine for children to be thus occupied. In warm seasons the work was performed on the porch or under the shade of a tree in the yard. Tourists saw spreads, robes, and rugs displayed from lines along the roadside. Competition hammered down prices. Reynolds says of this home industry that "many a woman worked at it for twelve to fourteen hours and received for her work a quarter of a dollar."

Welfare workers and labor organizers were powerless to attack this system of economic slavery in the home. But relief and stabilization were to come somewhat suddenly and dramatically through a threefold combination of forces. These were national legislation on wages and hours, the substitution of multiple-needle chenille machines for human fingers, and the establishment of bedspread houses with regularized employment practices, including bus transportation for workers. Professional designers were brought in to improve the color schemes. Spreads continued to be made in homes but by the new machine methods. However, the established "houses" had the larger share of the production when wartime shortages and priorities slowed down this industry.

The bedspread houses naturally resumed and expanded operation immediately after the war. Early in 1946, "Spreadcraft, Incorporated" moved into Cave Spring, Georgia, with twenty-four chenille machines and broke that sleepy little town's long-standing taboo against industry. This center of springs and caves had been a fashionable resort for planters before the Civil War. It continued to cater to aristocrats and to oppose any industrial invasion until World War II and bedspreads brought a change.

The improvised and artistic workmanship of a mountain woman was to lead to an annual business equal to half the cotton crop of Georgia, maybe more in postwar years. She started something.

The industrial revolution in the hill country furnished an outlet for rural labor in "public works," such as ore mines, rock quarries, logging and lumbering, construction of various types, and railway maintenance. A high proportion of this work was performed by common laborers who did chores which were already being largely handled by mechanical equipment in the North and West. They worked for wages that hovered around a dollar a day into the first years of the present century. The purchasing power of these wages was often reduced by the operation of a company commissary, which sold merchandise on credit within the amount of accrued wages and considerably above the range of fair cash prices. The commissary sometimes advanced cash or purchased workers' "time" before pay day at a discount resembling an annual interest rate. Railroad section workers used to refer to a commissary rigged up in a moving car as "the grab."

Section crews on the railroad worked long and hard in my boyhood days for ninety-five cents a day, with "section houses" for those having regular employment. The section foreman in those times received about forty dollars a month, and the supervisor of the division was ever telling him of more things to do. Inexperienced country boys had difficulty in measuring up to the task. Seasoned workers sometimes gave out, or "white-eyed," when the sun got hot in summer time. Negroes were not immune from this experience, as George Snow a few times exemplified under my observation. He was a fast and able worker. He was large and husky and could split a barn-side plank, by running at it and butting it, without hurting his head. He just had to lay down the shovel at times and seek the shade, even if fellow workers embarrassed him by kidding him for "white-eyeing."

There were buddies of George Snow who were observed to walk with a stiffness of hips and joints after a few years of "following public works." Sharecroppers who quit farming for industrial employment at common labor showed a physical change which landowners noted as an argument for lower pay for farm work. Bill Martin, a farmer in my community, once quit a temporary crosstie-cutting job, saying to the employer, "I'll work for you again for bread but never for meat." He would partly starve before he would work so hard for so little.

There were customs and even laws against the outside recruiting of laborers already regularly employed, against "enticing" them to quit a job they had "contracted" to work at. This policy had an agricultural background, and it was a feature of the transition from slavery. It might come into play in times or places of labor shortage, and it was often strengthened by the fact that workers lived in company houses, with implied or legal restrictions on certain types of visitors. Recruiting representatives were told to leave town, and occasionally more persuasion than talk was used. I could cite a cotton-mill case in which an interviewer was physically escorted out of town and told to keep going. Union organizers were later to meet this type of treatment in a more militant form.

It was a different story when slack times came, when a fly-by-night company picked up machinery and moved, or when a branch plant was discontinued by its Northern owner. It took Anniston some years to recover from the dismantling of a foundry by the American Car and Foundry Company, and Decatur, another Alabama town, experienced a similar backset when the L. and N. Railroad removed its shops. Employees scattered, some of them back to farms, and many merchants lost accounts.

There was a lighter side to rural "public works," in spite

of the long hours and hard labor. There was singing on the job, especially by Negroes. There were ways of initiating a new employee, perhaps by "giving him Lindy," which meant a paddling. Four men might take the newcomer, each by an arm or leg, and bump his buttocks several times against a tree. There was the stunt of sending a greenhorn here and there on a run-around for a "left-hand monkey-wrench." Teamsters on a road-grading or ore-hauling job used to send idle boys up and down the line for borrowing or retrieving a set of "cluckers." A Possum Trot boy, making several inquiries and walking two miles on such an errand before becoming disillusioned, decided to buy fifty cents' worth of stick candy at the commissary and get it charged to the man who started him on the phony jaunt. He returned with the purchase reporting it as the "cluckers."

The industrial employees normally had more money than farm workers for holiday excursions, weekend spending, whiskey drinking, and dice shooting, which was a frequent pay-day indulgence among both white and colored. There was a coined phrase, "The dice-shootin'est man I ever saw." Sometimes there were raids on gambling parties by "the law," with fines to be paid or worked out. In Alabama the lawbreaker might be sent to a coal mine in the Birmingham area under the convict-lease system, which was not ended until July, 1928. The practice was officially abolished only after long and ardent campaigning by reformers, including Julia Tutwiler, an educator, and Julia Russell, a farmer's wife. Mrs. Russell referred to the leaders of a convict mutiny at the Banner Mine as heroes performing God's work in risking their lives "in order to let the dull minded see what was being tolerated by the people."

The convict-lease system was maintained for those many years in Alabama as a source of revenue and of cheap labor. It was a definite check to the movement to organize the coal miners of the area, a check which was reinforced by the use of Negro strikebreakers when unionization seemed to be making headway.

The lot of convict miners was generally harder than that of other miners and other convicts. I well remember spending a day in the convict camp at Flat Top Mine out from Birmingham. It was a dreary scene. I remember the faces and the tired legs. There was also sickness in camp, and the only wall adornment for the patients to see was a sign that said, "Positively no profanity allowed. We don't give a damn ourselves, but it sounds like hell before company." There were exceptions to the hard life. It was in the time of state prohibition and prior to the national "noble experiment." The warden pointed to a prominent bootlegger from my country and remarked, "We let that fellow go to Birmingham one night and he came back with eight gallons of liquor."

When I naively asked if they took it away from him, the warden casually answered, "We helped him drink it up."

The industrial ways of work in the hill country were largely concerned with turning out cheap or coarse products down through the first World War. There was a concentration of employment in industries that yielded a low return per worker. There was not much making of fine cloth, high-grade equipment, automobiles, or clothbound books.

Lower Piedmont Country

The region had not yet moved extensively into quality production and the use of highly skilled labor. That meant hard work and low pay for workers moving from farm to town. Moreover, many workers had to move from the farm, for children were the biggest hill crop. Rural families were large, good acres were limited, and many members had to leave home, wanted to leave home as the years rolled along.

11

Ups and Downs Between World Wars

MANY a common man of the hill country made money for the first time in the decade of the first World War. The years just before the outbreak of hostilities in Europe were good for farmers, and even sharecroppers took on an air of independence. In that period I checked on the earnings of a group of farm tenants and croppers by interviews and store accounts. Without exception every one was paying his debts in the fall and having something left, the amount "cleared" ranging from twenty-five to two hundred dollars.

Many farmers, including tenants, were using bank credit and buying supplies for cash instead of having furnishing merchants charge them marked-up prices for goods "on time." There were farmers who were far enough ahead to pay cash without having to borrow. These had other products besides cotton to sell through the year, and they practiced thrift to make the money last. I heard a farmer's wife tell one of her children to wait a while before buying something, saying, "I don't have any change and I'm not going to break that ten-dollar bill just to spend fifty cents. The bill will soon be gone if I break it."

Prices of farm lands and farm products were "looking up," and the profit motive was abroad. There was talk about scientific farming and diversification to reduce the effects of boll-weevil damage. Some were hearing and reading about the agricultural teachings and demonstration work of Seaman A. Knapp, and a few youngsters were proving to their elders how much more corn could be produced on one acre. County agents were appearing on the scene, and railroads were sending out experts to preach better farming, sometimes furnishing a laboratory of agriculture on wheels. Hillbillies, however, opposed the compulsory application of science. Some of them were as obstreperous as their cattle on the subject of dipping the animals to prevent or eradicate the "tick fever." They slowed up the process of treatment by dynamiting dipping vats, which had been constructed to interfere with their liberties and convenience.

On the cultural side, county high schools and consolidated schools were spreading in the hills. There were examples of college students coming from backwoods homes of Hardshell Baptists. Motion pictures were showing in the larger towns, but frequently they had to respect religious opinion and avoid competition with the churches by not operating on Sunday. There were automobiles to scare country horses and to get stuck in the mud in rainy weather. Times were changing.

The President was Woodrow Wilson, a native of the Southern up-country who had practiced law in Atlanta and found him a wife at near-by Rome. When Mrs. Wilson died in the White House and was buried at Rome, throngs from the hills witnessed the funeral procession as it followed a horse-drawn hearse to Myrtlewood Cemetery. Birmingham's Oscar Underwood was one of the big men in Congress in making legislation for a new day. The Democrats were in power, and one of my schoolmates became a doorkeeper of the House of Representatives. My prosperous hill country was a part of the United States as never before.

The starting of war in 1914 upset the applecart of farm prosperity by temporarily wrecking the foreign market for cotton. But cotton came back into its own, and its price by the end of the war was over forty cents a pound, the highest in fifty years. Many hill farmers also found good wartime money in hogs, while the women went to town with such products as chickens, butter, and eggs. Industrial production jumped upward with plants turning out shells and other supplies for carrying on the war. That meant boom times and big employment for the mines and steel mills of the Birmingham district. At the same time workers from the hills sought higher wages in Northern centers, including a city they called "Deetroit." Many farm boys, white and colored, found themselves in the army with more pay above "board and keep" than they had ever known at home. Yankee soldiers trained in camps in the Piedmont region, spending their money and griping about winter weather in the "sunny South."

The war's end brought another cotton "panic" and another slump in the heavy industries in the early nineteen twenties. Birmingham had a heavy dose of unemployment, coupled with begging, thievery, robbery, and heavy night duty for policemen. With substantial help from outside the South, the Federal Reserve Bank of Atlanta carried extensive loans for member banks, slowed up on collections, and kept pressure off of borrowers in general until business men and farmers could get out of the woods. M. B. Wellborn, governor of the Atlanta Reserve Bank, had to fight within the reserve system for this lenient policy, but he was himself a banker from the North Alabama hills and he refused to make hard times harder. A certain amount of prosperity came around the corner by 1925. The up-country got a late and short exposure to the fabulous twenties.

Mules remained the chief source of plow power, but a few tractors were appearing on upland farms. Cultivators and other new machinery came along to replace lost labor and departed croppers. There were farmers who bought too much newfangled equipment for their own good, and some of it did not suit the fields and patches on steep hillsides. A tractor turned over in a mountain field near Possum Trot and rolled down through woods and rocks with such a crashing noise that fellows down in the hollow said they thought the world was coming to an end.

The hill country was moving forward in the development of electric power. Production of electricity between 1920 and 1930 doubled in Tennessee and Georgia and trebled in Alabama, with wide aid to industry and to the conveniences of living. Favorable conditions encouraged this development, which was greater than that in the rest of America. In the first place, the region has abundant coal for fuel-power plants. But a more important factor is its range of possibilities for hydroelectric power. It has mountains towering above its hills, and as much rainfall on these highlands as is to be found anywhere in the United States. Rivers rising in these mountains make rapid falls between rocky ridges to reach the plain and the sea. This provides ample and great opportunities for dams, artificial lakes, and water power to make electricity, as the United States government realized when it constructed Wilson Dam on the Tennessee River during the first World War and launched the giant TVA program on that river and its tributaries in the first term of Franklin D. Roosevelt. This Southern highland country has water power resources unsurpassed east of the Rockies and south of the New York and St. Lawrence region.

The private power companies turned heavily to hydro-electricity in the twenties. By 1930 ninety-nine per cent of the electricity produced in Alabama was from water power. So was ninety-three per cent in Georgia and sixty-eight per cent in Tennessee. Subsidiaries of the Commonwealth and Southern Corporation were busy with this development in three states. Over in the Carolina Piedmont, Buck Duke was making another fortune by this method after having made one as a tobacco magnate. The Aluminum Company of America undertook to make electricity at river dams for its own use in manufacturing in the Southern mountain country. The development brought many political issues to the front, with Senator George W. Norris insisting on holding the line against turning the government's Tennessee River projects over to private interests. Power companies became important in state lawmaking and government in the South.

The Southern Piedmont section had a big expansion in textile manufacturing in the era of Harding, Coolidge, and

Hoover. It took the lead in this industry from New England, where labor regulations and organizations were more effective. But the general industrial employment was never quite adequate for all those who were trying to leave the farm. Income on the farm seemed ever to fall behind income in business or industry, whether for workers or owners. There was plenty of dissatisfaction among rural people and small townsmen.

There were racial frictions in the hill country during the unsettled years immediately following the first World War. Race feelings were known in hamlets and cities, but were frequently intense in communities of declining status and opportunity. Certain whites had disturbing fears over claims that might be made by Negro veterans who had served in France. They repeated a made-up story of a conversation between two colored men. One was "going to get a white suit of clothes, white shoes, white socks, white shirt, white tie, and white hat, and have a date with a white girl." The other replied that he was going to "get a black suit, black shoes, black socks, black shirt, black tie, and black hat, and go to your funeral." Bootleg liquor frequently stimulated the friction.

The Ku Klux Klan was revived and organized on a new basis with headquarters in Atlanta. It undertook to "put the Negro in his place." It supported immigration restriction. It attracted Protestants, many of them believing what Henry Ford was publishing against the Jews and what Tom Heflin or Tom Watson was saying against the Catholics. In local instances it played a vigilante role against bootleggers and immoral joints, warning them at night with a fiery cross or using stronger measures. It was anti-communist and sometimes down on "labor agitators." At the same time there were rural Klansmen who politically opposed the big-business preferences of "city slickers." They opposed Al Smith, some actually believing his election as President would bring the Pope permanently to Washington. Finally, in Alabama, they turned against Oscar Underwood, who was friendly to business and disliked prohibition.

The Klan was opposed and exposed by the press in its own bailiwick. Julian Harris, son of the "Uncle Remus" writer, won a Pulitzer prize crusading against it with his Columbus, Georgia, *Enquirer*. Birmingham and Chattanooga, as well as Atlanta, had papers that frowned on the movement. The Klan worked on reporters of unfriendly papers, even roping them into the organization to check the effectiveness of their reporting. This in time facilitated final exposure. One reporter, for instance, as he explained to me, joined under pressure and gave inside information to another for use in a series of articles.

Countering the Klan's approach to race relations, a group of Southerners in 1920 organized the Commission on Interracial Cooperation, which like the Klan, had its main office in Atlanta. Will W. Alexander, a Methodist minister educated at Vanderbilt University, became its executive director. The organization embraced members of both races and both sexes, including editors, educators, religious leaders, social workers, and business men. It conducted investigations into the causes, patterns, and consequences of lynching, discovering and emphasizing that a large majority of the cases have no connection with rape. It sponsored an organization of

Southern women to prevent lynching. This group headed by
Mrs. Jessie Ames, of Atlanta, told Southern politicians that
Southern white women did not want lynching for their protection. These women turned the heat on local law-enforcement officers in critical situations. Mrs. Ames opposed national anti-lynching legislation, but called urgently for home
solutions of the problem.

This commission extended its membership over the South
and encouraged state committees to work at the race problem. It applied the teachings of conservative religion to this
human issue. It sought to bring whites and Negroes together
in mutual helpfulness as a continuing process. It was based
on a get-together spirit, which Atlanta had demonstrated
once before, in 1906, to restore calm after an inflamed race
riot. It was distinctly a factor in the reduction of lynching in
the South. It put out popular information about Negro
achievement since the days of slavery. When the Great
Depression became severe it moved into the farm-tenant
problem, serving both races, and its director became for some
years the head of the Farm Security Administration. During World War II the Commission has been transformed
into the Southern Regional Council for a broader attack
on Southern problems, including those of providing equal
opportunity for the Negro in school, on the job, and at the
polls. The Council has a special director of veterans' services.
This organization cooperated with other groups and leaders
in spiking numerous rumors and moderating race tensions
in the war period that followed Pearl Harbor. The Atlanta-
Birmingham-Chattanooga country held wartime racial feelings and incidents in check more successfully than did a

few congested centers or districts farther north or farther south, thanks to experience in handling the color line.

The Hoover depression hit the heavy industries of the hill country early and hard. Times were also gloomy for farmers, especially for those who were entirely dependent on cash crops for payment of debts. Some got by with the most rigid economy, as did a four-mule farmer near Jacksonville, Alabama, whose total purchase of hardware and equipment for making a crop consisted of four scooter plows for a total cost of less than two dollars. There were efforts to grow more food for home consumption, with reliance on home-made equipment as of old. For shelter, farmers rived boards by hand instead of buying roofing material. As hard as life was on the farm, stranded industrial workers were trying to get on the land as tenants, indebted owners or "squatters."

Birmingham leaders became particularly interested in locating unemployed workers on the land, and when the New Deal got under way four community projects of subsistence homesteads were located near that city in Jefferson County, with an additional one in the adjacent Walker County. The name of Senator Bankhead, who lived in Walker County, was attached to the act which provided for staking tenants or potential farmers to land ownership with financing by the Federal government. This measure had initial backing by the Commission on Interracial Cooperation. It was supported by the Southern Policy Committee of liberals and laborites, who organized in Atlanta in the spring of 1935 to publicize the region's need for progressive planning and action. As the first chairman of this group, I went to Washington to lobby for farm-tenant legislation.

The rural rehabilitation program of the Farm Security Administration had strong support in the Southern up-country. This work was started in 1934 with relief funds. It had the blessings of Harry Hopkins, who attended a conference in Atlanta for launching the venture, which was to become the main feature of a permanent agency dedicated to the welfare of small tillers of the soil. At the beginning thousands of hillbillies were transferred from relief lines to a contractual status as producers with enough equipment and supplies to make a living and pay their own way. The program suited semi-independent share tenants better than it suited croppers, who are completely dependent upon landlords. It appealed more to the up-country than to the low country, where opposition in time developed. It provided new incentives and gave the lie to the easy generalization that farm tenants are fundamentally "no 'count" and hopeless. There were no rural upheavals in the Piedmont like the sharecropper disturbances in Eastern Arkansas or in the "Bootheel" section of Missouri.

The rural rehabilitation program, with its material aid and emphasis on diversification, was to result in more food production by small farmers in urgent war years. It required written leases and added a bit of dignity and democracy to landlord-tenant relations. In spite of human, financial, and administrative limitations, it fulfilled much of the hope and vision with which it was inaugurated. It has been strongly supported by the Farmers' Union, though opposed or criticized at times by Southern leaders of the Farm Bureau Federation, with which planter interests are more closely linked. The basic human philosophy of the program is confirmed by a venture in family education for better farming at the Rabun Gap-Nagoochee school in North Georgia. Here children attend regular classes, while their parents learn farming and home-making as share tenants on school lands, frequently "graduating" to farms of their own. Farm tenants respond to the process of rehabilitation when given a fair and even chance under able and sympathetic leadership.

The TVA stands out among the depression agencies or activities of government for its effect on life in the hill country. It provided high-grade employment at times and places of most need. It switched many small farmers and one-horse tenants from kerosene lamps to electricity at rates that they could pay. I have seen TVA light in sharecropper homes. The man-made lakes of the Tennessee Valley, with new opportunities for fishing, boating, and picnicking, have been freed of malaria and mosquitoes by TVA scientists. The lakes reduce floods and remove or reduce the necessity for poor people to move away from incoming waters in Valley towns and cities. The improved navigation has brought in new industries, such as grain mills and elevators, while cheap and abundant power has attracted various types of manufacturing, including chemical and aluminum plants in wartime. With his mind on aluminum, aviation, and other war products, the late Senator Norris once said that TVA saved England. Oceangoing tugboats were made at Decatur, Alabama, during the war, and moved downstream to the Gulf and various parts of the world.

TVA has made an impact on labor relations with its construction-worker contracts, good wage policies, provisions for health and housing, and attention to such matters as education and recreation. At the same time it has maintained a merit system and avoided spoils or patronage in its choice of employees. It has affected farmers and farming with its program of cheap fertilizer, conservation, and demonstration practices, as well as through providing electricity for rural cooperatives. Only a small proportion of the families it displaced in lake areas were left stranded, dissatisfied, and unadjusted in a changed region. It has touched local government in numerous ways, as in power contracts, lease of park lands, and providing technical assistance. It has made the Valley tourist-minded by attracting hundreds of thousands of visitors to view the changed landscape.

The TVA dams have been built. The drama of big construction and big payrolls is about over. Many communities of the great Valley have shaken off the crust of isolation and made contact with the world. The TVA tasks that lie ahead are largely in the field of operation, maintenance, and development, including the development of industry, farming, and outdoor recreation among the people. Changing the level of living is a more difficult process than changing the level of the water that moves through the Valley. The river system has been speedily regimented for useful purposes, and this regimentation has made the income per capita rise proportionately more in the Valley than in the rest of the South. But the human system, not being subject to regimentation, requires time and patience to appreciate the new advantages and move voluntarily to a more abundant life. This point is recognized with clarity and hearty sympathy by David Lilienthal, chairman of the TVA directors, in his challenging book, *TVA: Democracy on the March*. This view inspires respect and response at Decatur, Guntersville, Chattanooga, and elsewhere in the up-country, by Chambers of Commerce as well as by local officials, farmers, and laborers.

The hill country had a greater part in World War II than in World War I. Its great resource of electric power was important, with three-fourths of TVA's output going to war plants. Its expanded textile mills served the war day and night. Its timber went to war, as did its mineral products. Its labor force moved into industry, learning new skills and earning new wages. This labor shift, combined with the drawing of many thousands into the armed service, reduced the population in rural counties which had no types of industries, war plants, or military camps. The military and industrial establishments brought in money, and, materially, there was greater good for a greater number than ever before. In spite of wartime rationing, the diet of many was much better than it used to be. In many ways this industrial part of the South boomed toward parity with the industrial North. Much of the farming made a change for the better, with less dependence on cotton growing and more production per man. Many sharecroppers, white and colored, found other ways of making a living, and many landholders found ways of farming without the use of sharecroppers. At the end of the war the Southern up-country was a different country and much concerned with problems of reconversion.

12

Possum Trot in Wartime

It is the second wartime year after Pearl Harbor and later. I am reporting from Possum Trot, my native bailiwick in the heart of the hill country. This North Alabama neighborhood is changing some of its ways because of the war, and it mirrors the changes of the region. I observe these changes as I make visits of a week and a month to this rural spot and ramble over the little valley, going to barn, and field and town with farmers, and gossiping with nearly everybody.

We had a turkey dinner—turkey in July—one of "Uncle Josh's" two turkeys which the foxes had not appropriated. "Uncle Josh" brought them in and said, "Eat 'em before the damn foxes get 'em." Prior to the war men imported young foxes and turned them loose in the woods to provide good hunting. But now the hunters have gone to war or to war work, and the foxes are devouring turkeys, chickens, and quail.

Many farm women are complaining about rabbits eating up young vegetables, for the men have less time and ammunition to shoot rabbits than in other days. Moreover, fewer acres of crops mean more brier patches and thickets for rabbits to live in and produce a surplus of wild meat for later times. Little pine trees are covering more of the land than at any time since 1900, and nature is rather freely taking its course. And Possum Trot is sure to have more possums when Hitler and Tojo are defeated.

I find only one sharecropper in this "neck of the woods," and he is not a regular sharecropper, since he gives part of his time to other work. Possum Trot has been full of sharecroppers, ranging from good to fair-to-middling and sorry. But sharecropping seems, like slavery, to have become outmoded.

There is little liquor or liquor-drinking in Possum Trot, nothing to compare with the drunkenness which I have seen here in former times. There are rumors, however, of wildcat stills back in the woods, with an occasional curl of smoke to confirm the rumor.

Possum Trotters are loafing and working more, drinking less and eating more, on the whole, than ever before. They have less row-cropping and hoeing but more hay-cropping and sowing. They have less cotton but more livestock and more poultry. The gin-house where I once weighed cotton is used to separate, clean, and store different kinds of hayseed. Farmers are actually treating cows decently on good pasture land. They cultivate fewer acres, but every family or household has income that is not farm income, largely from earnings from following "public works," or activity as "defense workers." Thus they grow food and buy food, and ration points give them little worry. One farmer did a truck-hauling job for a working family, and they paid him in accumulated rationed sugar.

Possum Trot used to sell cotton and timber to the outside world. But now it sells labor to the outside world. There is abundant opportunity for work outside the neighborhood, for this place is in Calhoun County, which is over fifty-per-cent urban, with Anniston as the county seat sixteen miles away. Fort McClellan in between offers civilian employment. Five miles beyond Anniston is "the dump," a munitions depot. Twenty miles to the west is Gadsden, with steel and rubber plants. There are other places to go, and these rural people are going.

Men of this community at one time found industrial work within walking distance of farm homes. There was work at saw mills, rock quarries, collieries, and cotton gins. As these opportunities slowed up or disappeared, many migrated to industrial centers far away. Now they just live at Possum Trot and streak out variously to distant work, like spokes from a hub.

The greatest hustler in the community is Lee Keith, a Negro share tenant, who owns five mules and good farm equipment and makes a good crop. He has a pick-up truck in which he travels to Fort McClellan for work daily, while members of his family work on the farm. Besides his own wages, he gets thirty-five cents from each of fourteen other workers for hauling them to and from Fort McClellan. He gets home early enough in the afternoon to put in farm work and look after things, also to collect and deliver washing. His family would make a good subject for a magazine article or poem or book. Other farmers have bought new equipment with money earned at carpentry or defense work.

At the other extreme from Lee Keith is the Hurt household of two doubled-up families, former sharecroppers. Eight of them are workers, three of them at farm labor, which enables them to have a farm-tenant house. Five of them go near and far to industrial work. One is a pipefitter at the Childersburg powder plant seventy-two miles away. To get there and back daily he drives a car to Anniston, parks his car, and joins a hook-up for the remaining fifty-six miles and back to Anniston, contributing a dollar to the hook-up, and coming home in his own car. The Hurts are neither saints nor money savers. Their money comes and goes. In the space of four months they bought and ruined or traded in a total of thirteen automobiles. Some months ago four of them got in jail at the same time. The others worked steadily and took in enough wages in a few days to get them out. Another time a group of them got in jail and got out without having to pay, for they were guilty only of being at a spot where some devilment happened. Two of them reported for the draft but soon came back. The Hurts are dynamic and cooperative. When they are together they can talk and do talk about work and goings on at Childersburg, Anniston, Jacksonville, and the dump, which seems to have enough war things to win a war.

The others who live in Possum Trot range in between the economic ways of Keith or the ways of the Hurts. Nearly everyone pays rent from wages earned somewhere else. One man and wife go off and work in a cotton mill, while their young children work on the landlord's farm to pay the house rent. "Snoocums" Herren, a Negro, works at the incinerator at the "Fort," and his wife does a little work for the landlord, for whom they used to be sharecroppers. "Snoocums" goes to and from work in his own nearly new Chevrolet, and every day he brings home a five-gallon can of slop from the "Fort" for his hogs. He takes the Pittsburgh *Courier.* His wife thinks spending is better than saving, and was heard to say that Hitler will wipe out our savings if he wins, and if we win we will have a revolution and not need savings. (On a later visit I learned that "Snoocums" and his family had removed to California.)

I counted nine farm tractors in the immediate vicinity of Possum Trot, and incidentally there were nine young men in the army in the middle of 1943. Several small farmers have adopted the practice of hiring tractor owners to turn land for them in winter or spring. "If I hadn't hired that bottom turned, I couldn't have got it planted," said Luther Whatley as he showed me his "brag" corn field, which was going to fill his crib.

The landholdings in beat eight, the precinct which includes Possum Trot, are smaller than they once were. The largest today is somewhat over seven hundred acres, the smallest one acre. Twenty years ago the range was from two thousand one hundred down to about forty. The county tax books show seventy-three landowners as local residents, with forty-six living outside the county. The non-resident owners are scattered from Gadsden to Ohio and even Minnesota, with inclusion of the Federal Land Bank of New Orleans, which took over farms for mortgages that could not be paid.

The number of dwelling houses is about the same as in earlier times. Many more houses show paint and screens than seemed possible a few years ago. Fewer people have chills and fever than in other years, and less quinine is consumed. Some of the tenants have sanitary privies, which came in with the New Deal relief administration. Two or three top-ranking farmers have running water in the home. Most of the residents use kerosene lamps, but quite a number have electricity, thanks to TVA. Any temporary increase in population is through the housing of more persons or families in one house. The community seems to fit the rural population picture of the whole Coosa Valley, which seemingly changed less than one per cent between 1930 and 1940. More families are now to be found along main highways, with fewer back "in the sticks" than there were before the era of the bus and automobile.

The number of qualified voters in beat eight seems to be about one hundred. This can not be exactly determined from the county records, which show no accurate write-off of permanent registrants who have left the state and not showed up in other Alabama counties. I found my own name on the list, with a war veteran's poll-tax exemption, though I have voted in other states for years. This number of one hundred is about the same as the precinct vote in 1896 in the bitter election campaign between Bryan and McKinley for President. White women have replaced disfranchised Negroes and poll-tax delinquents to keep the poll list fairly constant.

Not only does Possum Trot have less time for drinking

than it used to have, it also has less time for religion, and fewer chickens are killed for dinner for preachers. Salem Church seems pretty dormant, and plans for a revival came to naught when I was there for a summer month. Even the Holy Roller faith seems to be on the wane, though it was on the rise a few years ago. Holy Rollers are switching to good wages, with overtime at work rather than at church. One of their local preachers, the only preacher in the community, got a job at the "Fort" as a carpenter. When he got fired for not being a carpenter, he got himself rehired as a carpenter's helper and held his job.

Possum Trot is talking less about itself and its people than in other days. It has less local gossip. There is less of neighbor keeping up with neighbor. Frequently a man cannot give the name of a family living a mile away. There is a sort of monotonous unconcern as to who a stranger may be. A farmer's wife died while I was in the neighborhood, and the news was received by different ones with the same casual attention that city dwellers might show to the death of a stranger in the next block or apartment building. The loss and lack of community spirit is greater among whites than Negroes, who have a school and a church in the same building.

There are few signs of racial feeling in Possum Trot except talk about race problems in the nation and in the world, about the big race riot in Detroit and the killing in that disturbance of Henry Wood, a Negro, who had been a sharecropper. Two of his relatives went north to the funeral on funds provided by white and colored. They brought back

a story of Henry's being an innocent victim of a police raid
on a pressing shop. He was trying to recover two suits of
clothes, one of them handed down from Freeman, a brother
who had died on the farm two years ago. They said that
he shouted, "These are mine," but

> Cops, "the law," came in a-shooting,
> Thinking Henry Wood was looting,
> Heeding not his ardent pleading,
> And they left him dead and bleeding.

Local whites had different views about Negroes going to
war. "Niggers" should be kept out of military service, for
the army should be for whites only. They should not be left
at home to hold good jobs but should have to face danger
like the whites or more so. One observer, whom ex-slaves
would have called a "po' white," figured that, one way or
another, some sort of justice for the Negro would come out
of it.

The main little cemetery of the neighborhood has ceased
to be exclusively a resting place for whites, since the nearest
graveyard for Negroes became filled and could not be expanded. I saw the grave of John Smith, a white man from a
mountain farm, two steps from the marker of Amy Gray, a
Negro sharecropper's wife for whom I had weighed out many
a pound of coffee, sugar, lard, and "snowbelly" meat in a
country store. Near to both I read the marker of John Maxwell, who for years made and sold corn liquor, on which
white and colored got drunk.

I heard arguments for and against labor unions, sometimes among members of the same family. Women as well as men were expressing opposing views about the carpenters' union and the CIO. One farm woman said she and her husband could not talk to his sister and the sister's husband about "labor," because their opinions were so strong and different.

I found Possum Trot people gossiping about the world and the ways of the world more than ever. They were talking about Hitler and "them Japs," about Russia and "Joe," about Roosevelt and Churchill. They were reading more daily newspapers than formerly, with a carrier delivery of the Anniston *Evening Star* and R.F.D. bringing a few papers from Atlanta and Birmingham. They were also getting news by radio. Workers brought in news from town and city. Soldiers, soldiers' wives, and soldiers' letters gave wider contacts.

The little community has become much less isolated and much less a community. Like many rural hamlets of the industrial up-country, it is not to be reconverted to its onetime status, for it was already yielding its identity when the war came. It was already yielding its sharecropper type of cotton farming. In the war period its inhabitants got further away from the one-crop cotton system, and they learned to go farther away from home for work and play. They now long for more income and for wider horizons, while the little horizon of Possum Trot is lost in the shuffle of the times.

This neighborhood, in a broad social sense, is virtually an aggregation of individuals, foot-loose and unattached in mind or feeling to any geographical or political center. They largely lack the consciousness of belonging. They offer problems for statesmen and leaders, problems of developing larger social substitutes for the multitudinous disappearing communities like Possum Trot, where people get together only when they take final position in the cemetery. This is the real task of reconversion.

13

Labor Stirs

ORGANIZED labor, with its leadership, has followed organized capital, with its leadership, into the hill country. But there was quite a time lag between the two movements. Cheap labor was often emphasized as a feature to attract new industries, which were more welcome than union organizers. The great masses of common laborers were to remain for a long time unacquainted with unions of any kind. Individualism, paternalism, company stores, and company houses for workers were long the prevailing features of the labor front. Some of this paternalism manifested a high note of good will and humanitarianism on the part of employers, while some of it was vicious and brutal, especially toward Negroes, in construction camps.

Donald Comer, of Birmingham, has been an example of the better type of old-fashioned employer. He has supported welfare legislation and practices, applying the gospel in his own mills. He helped to organize and start the farm-tenant rehabilitation program in Alabama. But he could not warm up to the idea that labor leaders could really feel more responsibility for his workers than he felt for these workers. He did not like to contemplate a John Lewis or a John Lewis man coming between him and his workers. I have heard denunciations of him by union organizers. I have heard him praised for his personal interest in his workers as individuals. An employee once described to me at length and with pride a visit by Comer to his home at noontime on a working day. The simple fare, with fresh vegetables, was to Comer's liking. Mill president and mill worker had "dinner" together, while the important official was being sought out to take head place at a luncheon with a group of directors. Why, thought many, should outside "agitators" come in and disturb such harmonious relations as Comer and his kind preferred?

Moreover, able and considerate labor leaders, like the late Steve Nance of Atlanta, realized that organizing the workers on a wide scale would be a hard and slow process as long as sharecroppers and farm laborers were numerous, increasing, and poorly paid. As these rural workers moved into industry, they seemed to like the wages they received, to appreciate the attitude of their employers, and to have little inclination to join unions or strike for higher wages. There is the story of a poor hill farmer who started to administer a thrashing to two daughters who brought home the first week's wages from a mill village. The pay, in his eyes, was too much for legitimate earnings and seemingly represented service of the devil.

The first unions were in the skilled trades. These craft unions sprang up in the older cities of the lowlands before appearing in the newer industrial centers of the up-country.

They were only moderately active and did not seek Negro members. When attempts were first made to organize industrial workers, Negroes were available for work as strikebreakers. But colored workers were in time admitted to membership in separate locals, and finally in certain unions they became full participants along with white men. When John Lewis put the United Mine Workers behind the movement for starting the CIO, Negroes enjoyed regular status in the new set-up, both as members and as officers.

There were significant strike failures on labor's record between 1900 and 1934, when a series of contests swept over the textile towns of the hill country. There were fierce struggles in the mines around Birmingham. In 1908 twenty thousand black and white miners of this area went on strike. But convicts were working, strikebreakers were brought in, additional deputy sheriffs were sworn in, and state troops were ordered to the scene. Killings were frequent. Governor B. B. Comer, a Birmingham industrialist, addressed a group of assembled miners and announced that the strike was over. Under pressure, the national officers of the union declared the strike ended, and defeated workers went back to the coal mines and company shacks.

There were various strikes in the months following the first World War, and a leader reminded a Birmingham audience that President Wilson admittedly had found labor more nearly right than capital. In the late nineteen twenties the American Federation of Labor made a drive to organize the factory workers of the Southern Piedmont, and a series of strikes spread through the region. Many of the strikers were non-union workers rebelling against pressure for higher productivity. The press, with a few notable exceptions, was unsympathetic. The Atlanta *Constitution* attributed the movement to outside trouble-makers and Communists, though conservative AFL officials were responsible for much of the activity. It editorialized on the South's industrial advantages and observed that "if Providence gives to the Southeastern region better working climate, cheaper power, and labor able to live equally with Northern and Eastern labor on somewhat lower wages, the Eastern complaints should be made to God and not to the Southern industrialists and workers." It trusted Southern industrial leaders to work out "real labor and social problems" on just and humane bases. Mark Ethridge, then with the Macon, Georgia, *Telegraph,* and George Fort Milton, of the Chattanooga *News,* were more sympathetic toward organized labor. Ethridge had little fear of the "menace of communism" in the South, and, like Milton, he warned against indifference to the cause of labor.

The Great Depression following 1929 brought unrest and keen fears of trouble to Birmingham, where there were extensive shutdowns in mines, mills, and furnaces. Communist organizers moved in and sought connections with various labor groups, urban and rural, white and black. They started a magazine, the *New South,* without giving it a party label. They rallied to the defense of the Negroes who were involved in the Scottsboro case. They emphasized the issues of civil rights for Negroes and sharecroppers. Alarm spread, and floggings occurred, also killings.

Along came the New Deal, with labor gains up and down the line and a contract between a big CIO union and United States Steel, the largest employer in the Birmingham district.

William Mitch, as state head of the United Mine Workers and the CIO, won respect from employers and public leaders as well as from his own unions by pursuing a straight policy of gains for labor without flirting with Communism and without fanning the issue of racial friction. Business picked up, and Birmingham's labor relations became relatively quiet.

But strife was ahead for near-by Gadsden, which had all the growing pains of a rapidly expanding industrial center, surrounded by rural traditions and no little rural poverty. The city had a Republic Steel plant, a new Goodyear Rubber plant, a cotton mill, and other enterprises. The industrial companies did not want unions, and many workers seemed willing to go along with anti-union policies. Gadsden officials and local county officials did not want unions. The Gadsden *Times* denounced outsiders for meddling in local labor matters. When Sherman Dalrymple, president of the International Union of Rubber Workers (CIO), came to Gadsden in June, 1936, his courthouse speech was cut short with the throwing of rotten eggs and tomatoes and the starting of fist fights. Law-enforcement officers gave the visitor no protection against verbal and physical rough treatment.

I spent two days in Gadsden in July of 1937 and interviewed many workers, including members of AFL unions, CIO unions, and Jimmy Karam of the company "flying squadron." Feelings were tense, and beatings were frequent, for, many employees, with company encouragement, opposed national unions. Some of the unions could not meet openly. The president of the AFL Central Labor Union emphasized solidarity by saying, "We are all union men, is the way we look at it in Etowah County, and whether a fellow belongs to AF of L or to CIO doesn't make a great deal of difference." The "squadron" member, who had been a college football player, spoke with burning earnestness of his loyalty to Goodyear and his opposition to the CIO, coercion, and Communism. He had come to Goodyear without money, had "worked like hell," and was accepted for work on the squadron. He said, "When you work on the squadron you have to weigh at least 160 pounds in order to work in every department of the plant. On the squad you are transferred from department to department until you learn the job thoroughly in every department of the plant." The squad members got good wages and seemed ever ready for emergency activity, which, organized workers said, included fighting the unions and union men.

Old ways and new ways clashed at Gadsden, as at Huntsville, Alabama, and other places in the decade of the nineteen thirties. It was the case of old paternalism *versus* new unionism, of local particularism *versus* national standards. Organized labor was insisting that big unions must accompany big business and that wages at Gadsden must equal wages at Akron or Cleveland. Employers and their supporters wanted to retain the lower wage advantage. Hence it seemed a crime to join a union, or it seemed a crime for a laborer not to join a union, according to who was speaking. But industrial Gadsden was soon to accept the Wagner act and labor unions in pretty good faith and to forget about Communistic fears.

"The Reds are taking her for a ride," said an Anniston banker when Mrs. Roosevelt was participating in the first

South-wide meeting of the Southern Conference for Human Welfare at Birmingham in November of 1938. The meeting was a mass effort to advance the rights, economic status, and general welfare especially of industrial workers, small farmers and farm tenants, and Negroes. It struck at regional differentials in wages, while Governor Bibb Graves led a panel discussion on freight-rate discrimination as affecting the South. It heard speeches or remarks by President Frank P. Graham, of the University of North Carolina, Justice Hugo Black, Senator Claude Pepper, and many others, including Mrs. Roosevelt. It circulated many hundred copies of the National Emergency Council's Report to the President, which analyzed the South as the "nation's number one economic problem." It handed out reprints of Jonathan Daniel's article, "Democracy Is Bread," which had recently appeared in the *Virginia Quarterly Review*. It challenged the *status quo* in various ways, praising the La Follette Civil Liberties Committee and condemning the methods of the Dies Committee on Un-American Activities. It supported the Roosevelt administration program in the fields of housing, social security, labor, and farm tenancy. It denounced the poll tax and called for Federal aid for education as well as a greater public program of "medical, dental and institutional care."

The leadership, membership, methods, and pronouncements of the conference were disturbing to the worshipers or adherents of Old South patterns of labor relations and race relations. It was noted that many Federal appointees were active participants. Among these were Judge Louise Charlton of Birmingham, who was the chairman, and Aubrey Williams, who headed the National Youth Administration. Williams had worked as a private employee in Birmingham, and his strong words for the underdog led to a national press report that he advocated a class struggle. The presence of half a dozen known members of the Communist Party was used as a basis of criticism within and without. A few bolted the permanent organization and lambasted it for its fellow travelers, rather overlooking the fact that the conference included many Catholics, some of them officially appointed. Others disliked the set-up because industrial laborites outnumbered business men and farmers and because the CIO furnished an important part of the membership as well as the support.

The outside opposition seized most avidly upon the biracial feature of the conference as contrary to the spirit and traditions of the South. There were about two hundred Negroes among the twelve hundred who had registration badges. They represented labor unions, newspapers, churches, universities, and various organizations. They had places on the program for the discussion of race relations and other issues. They were at the city auditorium in full force for the first session on Sunday evening when Frank Graham proclaimed "our stand for liberty, democracy, and the right of autonomous organization" and denounced repression, "whether it be of the Negro, Catholic, Jew, or laborer." This was an inspiring keynote address to a heterogeneous and hopeful audience. For comparison, it sent my memory back to a seat in the gallery at Chicago in the summer of 1912 when the Progressive Party convention nominated Theodore Roosevelt for a comeback term as President to advance the cause of " a nobler America." A member of the group on the platform with Graham was impressed by the capacity crowd of white and colored and remarked, "This audience is significant. It is the end of the Old South." His words had a touch of prophecy, but he said a little too much too soon.

The race issue came to a head suddenly and dramatically the next day. On this Monday afternoon I was presiding over a large sectional meeting in the auditorium on farm tenancy. For speakers I had rounded up Donald Comer, Dr. Wilson Gee of the University of Virginia, Dr. Charles S. Johnson of Fisk University, and representatives of the Farm Security Administration, the Farmers Union, and other groups. When we were about two-thirds through the program, the general chairman arrived and called three or four of us to a side room and informed us that "hell has broken loose." Police officers were ready with orders to take immediate action if we did not then and there apply racial segregation to the seating of the audience. We stopped the speaker and reshuffled the crowd with the central aisle as the dividing line. When we came back in the evening to hear Mrs. Roosevelt, one side of the auditorium was prominently marked for "Colored." On the following day the police complained of failure to observe legal segregation at a panel discussion in one of the churches.

Soon after the permanent organization was perfected and the members departed local politicians arranged a special mass meeting and roundly denounced the Southern Conference for Human Welfare. The next general session was held at Chattanooga, with Frank Graham as chairman. Subsequently Clark H. Foreman of Atlanta was to become active as general chairman. The main office was located at Nashville, the executive secretary being James Dombroski, a product of Emory University and a former member of the staff of the Highlander Folk school, an institution for workers at Monteagle, Tennessee. Labor and Negro groups continued to support the organization and its work for broader political and civil rights for all.

The Southern Conference for Human Welfare expanded activities in wartime, sponsoring publications as well as meetings in Atlanta and other cities. It has given hearty support to labor unionism, suffrage reform, the Farm Security Administration, and the removal of discrimination in employment practices. At the same time the organized labor movement has grown rapidly in the hill country, as in other regions of the South and the nation. Atlanta, for many years a regional center for the AFL, has likewise become an important headquarters point for the Southern activities of the CIO. In the field of public relations, important work for the CIO in the Southern region has been carried on for some years by Miss Lucy Randolph Mason, who came to Atlanta from her native Virginia. She speaks as a direct descendant of George Mason, the bill of rights pioneer of revolutionary times. Having an aristocratic and religious background, she champions the cause of labor with immunity from charges of being an uninformed or atheistic outsider. George S. Mitchell, a native Southern economist with college teaching experience, served for a time in Atlanta as regional director of the CIO's Political Action Committee. He is a co-author, with Horace R. Cayton, of a large book, *Black Workers and the New Unions.*

Labor leaders are endeavoring in different ways to accommodate themselves and their movement to Southern ways and views. George Googe, general AFL representative in the region, at times gives expression to traditional ideas of anti-radicalism. I have heard AFL union men criticize the Southern Conference for Human Welfare.

Many up-country employers now accept organized labor and collective bargaining in good faith. One of these is the TVA, which maintains a master contract with AFL unions, all jurisdictional disputes being handled by a labor council. But the hill country, with all its new industries and new payrolls, is far from being highly unionized. Unions are still looked upon in many quarters as unnecessary or as agencies of evil. There are numerous small and middle-size establishments without organized workers or labor contracts. Rural sawmills often fall into this class. Many industrial workers are common laborers who have social security cards but not union cards. The Fair Labor Standards Act, with its wage and hour provisions, protects many Southern laborers who have no union connection. As a result of wartime expansion, there are cases of a single family of non-union workers bringing home an annual total pay of ten thousand dollars and more. That is new money and big money in the eyes of rural-minded people of the hills. World War II put scores of thousands of up-country families into the national picture of wages and income. It placed many Negroes in a new scheme of economic existence.

National unions recognize this new development and, with it, the possible opportunity for a continued drive to organize the unorganized. A sort of union evangelism is abroad in the land. It must move against a rural individualism, which remains strong when it goes to town, to school or to church. The hills are true to the old saying that "You can get a man out of the country, but you can't get the country out of him." The race problem is also a difficulty for organized labor, though earnest efforts are made to overcome it. The high birth-rate, with accompanying areas of poverty, also checks the labor movement in the region, and there are Southern economists who use population and poverty as arguments against high wages and labor controls, whether by unions or government. For the long pull, however, organized labor has the advantage of the expanding industrialism of the uplands, where new electricity, new capital, and other new factors are removing frontier conditions.

14
Piedmont Politics

THE INDUSTRIAL hill country stands out in a political landscape of imbalances and inequalities, with an uneven distribution of public power between sections, between races,
and between economic groups. Political molds made long
ago have to be used in the South in making new policy for
labor relations and social welfare. The new wine of social
progress has to be contained in old political bottles. The up-
country's democratic power in public affairs has not kept
pace with its economic development and its population
growth. It was once inferior to the lowlands in wealth, productivity, and population figures. But it is now ahead on
these scores, and a man of the hills might view the economic
changes with a feeling no longer of bottom-rail inferiority.

Such a statement, however, would not apply to politics,
whether in Alabama, Georgia, Tennessee, or several other
Southern states. In the whole region from the Virginia Tidewater to the Mississippi Delta agrarian gentlemen arrived
early, established priority of power, and later exercised con-

trol out of proportion to their numbers. Their dominant influence was felt in the days of slavery and secession, in the "bourbon" rule following Reconstruction, and in the writing of state constitutional clauses to restrict voting and reduce the threat to the "solid South" by Populists and Republicans, including Negroes. It is felt today when the labor movement is showing strength among both races and demanding a wider suffrage along with repeal of the poll tax as a requirement for voting. This condition of unbalanced power furnishes a hedge against democratic trends in the hills and elsewhere. It distorts the picture of the real South, which is inherently not nearly so reactionary as the role of many Southern leaders at Washington would indicate.

Since time immemorial the lowland advantage has shown up most strikingly in state legislative apportionment. The pattern set by the Virginians has been followed by other states. Tennessee has a legislative apportionment that fits the state's distribution of population according to the census of 1900. The state constitution calls for reapportionment every ten years, but this provision is not followed. Republican leaders and industrial centers of East Tennessee complain but get no action. The Crump machine of Memphis, with various rural county connections, exercises strategic power in Tennessee government and politics. The Delta on the West is more dominant than the Highland on the East in the affairs of the Volunteer state.

The people of Atlanta are close to disfranchisement in the political life of Georgia. Their county of Fulton has one of fifty-four state senators. This county has one-eighth of the state's population, but just three of more than two hundred members of the state house of representatives. Yet Echols County, on the Florida border, has less than three thousand inhabitants by the 1940 census and one state-legislative representative. Georgia is a leading state in small rural counties, as in the number of moonshine stills, and most of its 159 counties have been losing population for many years. But they have retained their legislative power. The legislators from Atlanta and other industrial centers of North Georgia are lost in a large group of rural colleagues. It was made that way at the end of the Reconstruction era by a constitutional convention which was dominated by Robert Toombs, a planter's son who wanted to lock the door to the state treasury and throw away the key. He treated Atlanta as roughly in the political sense as did Sherman in warfare. Most of his handiwork remains.

Georgia's disproportionate rural supremacy is carried over into Democratic primaries by legislative provisions for using county units in the nomination of state officers, state judges, and United States senators. The candidate winning a county plurality of the popular vote gets the units of that county. The units vary from two to six per county, with the total running to 410. Three small counties can cancel out Atlanta's Fulton County. An Atlanta voter has only a fraction of the electoral power of a rural voter in state primaries, with a majority of the units being required to choose a governor or United States senator and only a plurality for other officers. Since the Democratic primary is the decisive election, the little counties largely run the show.

This Georgia unit system reinforces the prevailing legislative apportionment to give excessive power to the rural vote. It may be argued that a "bold peasantry, their country's pride," casts a good vote and properly deserves more voice than "city slickers." But it is not healthy to rely heavily upon the wishes of people in rural counties and communities which are falling behind in income and population and are losing a large proportion of their active and productive adults. Many of the persons who are left behind in such areas are highly susceptible to demagogic appeals to prejudice and passion on the grounds of race, class, or outside interference. This is well recognized by demagogues, by Gene Talmadge, who calls himself a farmer and hails from a small town in South Georgia. In reducing the voting age to eighteen this state met a need, greater than anywhere else in the Union, to offset the power of a rural aged electorate.

My native Alabama has had no state legislative reapportionment since the present constitution went into effect in 1901. Yet that constitution contains a clear provision for a redistribution every ten years. The picture is not so lopsided as in Georgia, since there are not half so many little counties with a declining population. But it is queer enough by the test of democratic government. That is strikingly clear from an analysis in a study by Dr. Hallie Farmer, *The Legislative Process in Alabama: Legislative Apportionment,* made in 1944 for the Bureau of Public Administration of the University of Alabama. The northern county of Jefferson, which contains the city of Birmingham, had nearly half a million inhabitants by the census of 1940 and has subsequently increased. But this sixth of Alabama's population is represented by only one of thirty-five state senators and seven of the 106 representatives in the lower house of the legislature. At the other extreme is Lowndes County down in the black belt with a population that had declined to 22,661 by 1940, three-fourths of the number being non-voting Negroes. Lowndes has one senator and two representatives. It takes many voters of Birmingham to equal one of Lowndes in legislative power at Montgomery.

This "rotten borough" system of representation in Alabama is a mixture of white supremacy, black belt supremacy, and rural supremacy. It is clearly unfair to North Alabama. The southern half of the state has less than half the population, less than half the wealth, and less than half the tax burden, but a majority of both houses of the state legislature.

The system tends to perpetuate itself, with men and regions that have power refusing to yield their advantage. Legislators from declining rural counties, including a few from North Alabama, oppose reapportionment and thus continue black-belt supremacy with an accompanying opposition to constitutional changes for liberalizing the suffrage. Reapportionment proposals have died in judiciary committees. A bill in conformity with the campaign pledge and urgent plea of Governor Frank M. Dixon, of Birmingham, reached a vote in the lower house in 1939, only to be defeated by sixty nays to thirty-one yeas. All but six of the yeas came from the North, and most of the nays came from the South.

The rigid and disproportionate composition of the legislature in these and other Southern states prevents it from being representative in any popular sense. It is likely to throw the lawmaking body out of line with the governor, unless a big patronage machine can gain harmony. The drastic state laws concerning labor unions are partly to be explained by unbalanced apportionments. Labor has much more cause than has capital to be disturbed over the under-representation of urban and industrial regions as well as over the poll tax and other restrictions on voting. The ancient Athenian type of limited democracy, which flavored the politics of the Old South, retains a certain vogue in modern days with the support of rural courthouse rings and country gentlemen. By nature and background it is not pro-labor.

The rural conservative elements of the lowlands do not work alone. They meet opposition at home and get support from the hills, often through an *entente cordiale* with corporate interests. The president of the Alabama constitutional convention of 1901, which did so much for black-belt supremacy, was John B. Knox, a highly successful railroad attorney from the upland city of Anniston. His fees came from a system dominated by the J. P. Morgan interests of Wall Street. One of the convention members was Tom Heflin, with his strong words about Negroes and about Yankees. While rationing voting, the convention also put rigid ceilings on taxation. Talmadge has received important support from the largest corporation officials of Atlanta for his rabble-rousing appeals to rural and racial prejudice.

The legislature, constitutionally packed in favor of the older rural regions, affects state government and state politics in various ways. Those regions get the edge in picking or controlling the governor, if not the United States senators. They get favorable consideration in the laying out of districts for representatives in Congress, often at the expense of the newer urban areas. Their leaders know something about the art of gerrymandering to check the power of the other sections. Henry N. Williams, a political scientist, shows this trend in a study of Tennessee. My native bailiwick in North Alabama is in the fourth district, which extends north and south through several counties in a row and includes the old Alabama River town of Selma. That old black-belt center much of the time furnishes the congressman and furnishes a conservative, as at the present time in Sam Hobbs. The adjacent fifth district makes a long curving sweep from Sand Mountain down into the low country, though an industrial population in the upper end has taken over control.

The industrial hill country came of political age too late for a large crop of old-fashioned orators of the rabid or romantic school. It has not produced a fire-eater like Tom Heflin or Tom Watson or Gene Talmadge or Huey Long or Theodore Gilmore Bilbo, though it has listened to such rabble-rousers and voted for them. The "Senator Claghorn" type comes not from the hills, but from the Deep South of lower altitudes, often from centers in areas where King Cotton became sick or the timber was cut away. The best-known eloquence of the new up-country has been associated with evangelists like Sam Jones or boosting publicists like Henry Grady rather than with official political leaders. The region has had middle-of-the-road politicians who substituted capitivating stories for burning issues, as did "Fiddling Bob" Taylor of East Tennessee. It has had its share of unheralded but stirring eloquence by lawyers before juries in murder trials.

The dynamic hill country has made governors and lawmakers out of bankers, industrialists, and corporation lawyers. It has elevated conservatives and progressives. It has produced such different types of political leaders as Oscar Underwood, B. B. Comer, Hugo Black, W. H. Felton, and Ellis Arnall, who temporarily reversed the Talmadge trend in Georgia. Atlanta, Birmingham, and Chattanooga particularly have congressmen who are pretty progressive and sympathetic toward organized labor. Mrs. Helen Mankin, an Arnall supporter who had the backing of the CIO and Negro voters, was chosen in Atlanta in February, 1946, to succeed the liberal Robert Ramspeck, who had resigned. Birmingham's Luther Patrick, an in-and-out congressman, has been a New Dealer, an opponent of the poll tax, and a public critic of Bilbo. Representative Estes Kefauver, of Chattanooga, has been a strong supporter of Roosevelt-Truman policies, an opponent of anti-labor bills, a supporter of Federal aid to education, and an advocate of plans for modernizing Congress. John Sparkman, a progressive from a North Alabama district, succeeded Ramspeck as Democratic whip in the House, and then won a Senate seat.

TVA's successful development and popularity add strength to the position of these social democrats, and they, in turn, stand by TVA, offering opposition to attempts to enmesh it in spoils and patronage. That great valley project alone, however, is not enough, either for the region's economy or for a progressive program. The late President Roosevelt is reported to have said as much to John Rankin in urging him to support other New Deal measures as he was supporting TVA. He reminded the North Mississippi Congressman that people cannot eat electric power. Joe Starnes, of Guntersville on the Tennessee, was defeated for reelection to Congress in 1944 and defeated again in 1946, in spite of his vigorous support of TVA. He had also been active as vice chairman of the Dies Committee on Un-American Activities and wanted to know of a WPA theater project witness if sixteenth-century Christopher Marlowe "is" a Communist. His district included the industrial center of Gadsden, and he lost to a labor attorney.

Conservatives or reactionaries continue to serve in Congress from the industrial up-country. An example is Carter Manasco, anti-administration chairman of the House Committee on Expenditures. He represents an Alabama district in which coal mining is an important industry. The hill country, as other sections of the South, has various shades of political opinion among its leaders and followers. The South, including the hills, is far from solid, and assumptions of complete and consistent conservatism for the region constitute a political myth. This myth was analyzed for what it is by William G. Carleton in the *Virginia Quarterly Review* for the spring issue of 1946. But it is true by a good margin that the up-country sends more progressives to Washington than do the lowland districts. It is more interested in national measures and generally less interested in harping on states' rights than is the Old South region. Governor Arnall, hitting at the reactionary view, says, "There has been too much prattle about states' rights and not enough about states' responsibilities."

The hill country is making political headway in realistically facing race relations as well as labor relations. It weathered the racial tensions, rumors, and frictions of World War II more successfully than other regions farther south or farther north. It has so far not witnessed such a Ku Klux Klan movement as followed World War I. Significantly Talmadge's race appeal failed to gain victory in wartime, though he made a close come-back in 1946.

Facing race relations politically, however, is not a smooth task. It goes against the pattern of white supremacy, a pattern which does not yield easily. It invites attacks from the quarters of the demagogues, so much so that a Southern political progressive occasionally finds it expedient to assert adherence to white supremacy, to fight fire with fire, or demagoguery with demagoguery. It is well known in informed circles that this technique has been practiced reluctantly. One prospective candidate, who had been associated with an organization for Negro betterment, said to me that he would start early with a traditional stand on the race issue to forestall an attack by a Negro-baiting opponent. The use of the issue by two groups seems easy as long as Negro voters are not numerous. However, it serves partly to retard and also to conceal the constructive progress being made in the sphere of race relations.

The race question is recognized in the hills as one that cuts politically into various problems, particularly employment, education, suffrage, and the Democratic primary. There are many white and Negro leaders who are working at the task of adjusting and improving race relations in the region. White and colored men and women, including editors, educators, and religious workers, are sitting down together and discussing this set of problems. Upland cities, especially Atlanta, have had such conferences. The members have frankly explored such matters as employment, education, and suffrage. They have considered what the South can and should do toward applying the United States Supreme Court decisions against state discrimination in educational opportunity and in party primaries, which are conducted and regulated under state law as part of the function of state government. The Southern Regional Council, with its office in Atlanta, is active through officers and directors of both races. The National Association for the Advancement of Colored People has chapters in the region. The work of the Southern Conference for Human Walfare has led Bilbo to denounce it as the South's enemy number one. The CIO has a good proportion of Negro members and officers in the industrial sections. The AFL, in launching a Southern membership drive in 1946 to match a CIO drive, emphasized an appeal to Negroes in an announcement by the regional representative, George Googe, of Atlanta. Labor unions and the Farmers Union have been behind state and national movements to abolish the Southern poll tax.

Labor was on the job at a bi-racial meeting in Atlanta in December, 1944, on voting restrictions, with attention to the poll tax, arbitrary registration procedure, and discrimination against Negroes in the Democratic primary. It was a conference of a Committee of Editors and Writers of the South. It was presided over by Mark Ethridge, of the Louisville *Courier-Journal,* once a Georgia newspaperman. It seemed significant on this occasion to hear Georgia editors, white men, come right out and say that Negro voters should participate in primary elections on the same basis as whites.

The issue of the "white primary" came to a decision in Georgia early in 1946. A Negro, Primus E. King, "a qualified and registered voter in Muscogee County," won a damage suit in Federal court against primary election officials for denial of the vote "solely because he was of the colored or Negro race." The decision was upheld by the United Circuit Court of Appeals, and the Supreme Court, which had upheld a Texas Negro's claim, refused to review the case. Governor Arnall indicated that he would not be a party to subterfuge and would not call a special session of the legislature to seek ways of circumventing the decision. Lon Duckworth, chairman of the State Democratic Executive Committee, stood with Arnall on the issue. Talmadge immediately went on the political warpath, and so did Roy Harris, a strong Talmadge man and speaker of the house in the Georgia legislature. On April 16, Harris, with his "Cracker party," met an overwhelming defeat in the Democratic primary election in Richmond County, in which Augusta is located. Whites as well as Negroes cast a majority against him. The long-standing issue of the role of the Negro in politics is far from settled, but new leaders have arisen to battle the old.

The Piedmont country in many ways is in the forefront in the process of whittling down the differentials which set the South off from the rest of the United States, differentials in race relations, labor relations, freight rates, general income, technology, and education. Negroes are getting a better deal in industry, education, and political affairs than formerly. Through the influence of unions and national legislation the wages and conditions of labor are moving toward equality with the North. Political leaders of the region are fighting for freight-rate parity with the North on the shipment of manufactured goods. TVA economists and officials

give support to efforts for breaking down this barrier on
Southern manufacturing, offering this step as a factor in increasing high-class production and income. Many up-country
congressmen and editors are asking for Federal aid for education without displaying the old fears of dictation and interference from Washington with state and local management.
They are more national in this respect than some of their
lowland colleagues. They are less wedded to the South's past.
The progressive forces of the hill country are more inclined
to look to Congress for salvation than to state legislatures,
where an antiquated apportionment supports the *status quo*.

Worshipers and beneficiaries of these differentials view
their disappearance with concern and alarm. Certain producers and shippers of cheap heavy freight, such as coal, enjoy favorable "commodity" rates and strongly oppose the
movement for reducing "class" rates on any uniform basis.
Many of the same interests oppose a higher minimum wage
law as well as regulation for fair employment practices for
Negroes. They are joined by groups who fear farmers will
be left behind without cheap labor and others who just see
Southern culture disappearing in a whirl of materialism.
With burning sincerity, a literary agrarian denounces labor
unions for emphasizing wages and hours and being a threat
to the Southern way of life. To him TVA is a centralized
imposition upon a region, with the substitution of Pennsylvania Avenue for Wall Street as the place of power. There
are Southern historians who take the South for their parish
and who view the present as another era of unfortunate "Reconstruction." A writer and wealthy planter of Georgia con-
siders Talmadge as not the worst evil and quietly says,

"Better a hundred Talmadges than one Arnall." There is concern in certain upper-class families who seek a scapegoat because there are no longer enough Negro domestic servants to carry on the traditional ways of the South.

World War II brought on increased attacks on this landscape of differentials, though it did not remove them and it did not abolish rural poverty on eroded hills. The Southeastern region, including mountains, valleys, and plains, remains the "seedbed of the nation," roughly accounting for one-third of America's population increase, though receiving only about one-eighth of the national income. As Rupert B. Vance says in *All These People,* Southerners, though having less on which to live, "are doing more to replace themselves in the next generation than any of the Nation's folks." People constitute the region's largest product, whether for home employment or for migration. The war temporarily bridged the gap between workers and jobs, between man and land, but it did not solve the problem of the Southeast's population growth, which invites national attention and explains why Kefauver and other congressmen favor Federal aid for public schools.

The war increased the number, proportion, and power of industrial employees in the region from the mountain to the sea. With political significance, it reduced the differences in wages within the South and between South and North. It spread labor politics more widely in urban and industrial sections. The expansion of industries and population in coastal districts tended to match the expansion of the hills, thus squeezing the lowland agrarians more decidedly into a minority group. In moving many sharecroppers off the land it brought more independence to the remaining tillers of the soil. The man on the tractor or cotton picker is likely to be different as a political animal from the average worker with the mule or hoe. This may make certain large level areas of the South resemble the West in public outlook. The increased diversification of farming in the hill country is tending to diversify the politics of that region. The war gave the South a large crop of war veterans, who are getting various types of aid from a generous national government without regional or racial discrimination. The lot of these is quite different from that of Confederate veterans after 1865. It is superior in terms of net economic welfare to the lot of the millions of Southern ex-slaves, whose excited hopes of "forty acres and a mule" were never realized.

These wartime developments are not ending the political problems of the Piedmont country. But they are changing the problems and placing them more clearly in the national picture, making them less peculiarly Southern. The selection in 1946 of "Big Jim" Folsom as Democratic nominee for governor of Alabama, with CIO support and small-farmer support, was an event which could not have happened in earlier days in that state. Here was a man from the hill country north of Birmingham advocating the abolition of the poll tax and defeating the leading candidate from the black belt. He campaigned with hillbilly music on a progressive platform and served notice that lowland dominance is not what it has been.

More than ever the industrial hill country is becoming like America's other industrial regions in the outlook of workers, managers, capitalists, and farmers. It is more widely acquainted with the ideas of social security and with the demands of modern society. The broad issues of social politics have come to this country, which might be called a Northern South and a Southern North.

15

The Mind of the Hills

━━━━━━━━━

WHEN the stars fell on Alabama and other regions in the President Jackson era, Nick Davis, the North Alabama political leader, was returning with his race horses to his Huntsville home from New Orleans races. The stars turned him from races to religion, and, as a good convert, he sold his horses, so as to put that type of wickedness behind him.

This story, preserved by Davis descendants, exemplifies the mind of the hills as it has been and, to a great degree, as it is today. That mind is influenced by living largely outdoors, having abundant contact with the workings of nature, and being exposed to violent types of weather. Associated with this influence is a fear of God as described in a literal Bible and interpreted by a strictly orthodox Protestant clergy. This fear has not been limited to church members, but it is part of the mental make-up of "unbelievers." It lends itself to specific applications, as when Nick Davis saw a divine warning in the falling meteors. A man died suddenly, and a Possum Trot neighbor said it was the Lord's way of punishing him for the way he acted in some land deals. An energetic farmer in the same neighborhood was greasing his wagon on Sunday and otherwise getting things ready for a good week's work. His wife told the children, in answer to questions, that the Devil would get him if he did not change his ways from Sabbath-breaking.

These awesome ideas are given variety and support by a body of superstitions, general and local, often believed by white and colored. There is a legend in Banks County in North Georgia that women who drink water from the Twin Spring, near the Broad River Church, are likely to have twins. Chemical analysis of water from this spring reveals nothing to explain twins, but local folk belief is to the contrary. Connie Watts, interviewed by an Atlanta *Journal* feature writer in March, 1946, attributed his own twin boys to that vein of water, which opens up among stones, moss, and ferns in a little hollow. He counted up to fifty families in the surrounding country who have had twins. It is observed that many modern women carefully avoid the spring because of its influence. But if twins are wanted, it is said that there is more magic in using a gourd to drink out of.

Two men once spent days vainly digging for gold supposedly hidden in a creek bank by Indians in a corner of my neighborhood. Their only clue was an old woman's dream, in which a man, long dead, appeared and gave information as to the treasure and its location. And then there were vivid accounts of the ghosts of local patriarchs walking at night, one of them being that of Jesse McCain, an ex-slave.

The hill people, on the whole, have not experienced physical and cultural changes of a sufficient degree to overthrow the traditional ideas handed down from frontier life and from times of the Great Awakening in the field religion. As rural people they had less immunity than many others from the effects of climate, heavy rains, and storms. Working, hunting, or idling at home, they have been in close contact with the elements. The houses have been relatively small, too often without ceiling, and so constructed as to be naturally cold in winter and hot in summer, making the inmates ever conscious of the Acts of God outside. With the passing of log cabins, many a hillside house has seemingly been built to sway with the howling wind and bring on feelings of earthly insecurity. Uneasy families have constructed storm cellars and used them. There have been times when I have wished for such a contrivance. Plantation architecture, with its impressive stability, made only a slight impact on the civilization of the hills except around a few old towns on the lower borders.

It is little wonder that old-fashioned thinking and feelings about religion remain strong among many of these people, especially among those with little book-learning. It is little wonder that the men of the hills were strong for William Jennings Bryan, the agrarian radical in his day in politics, and later were likewise strong for Bryan, the religious conservative and arch foe of the satanic theory of evolution. It was natural and symbolical that the prosecution for teaching the doctrine of evolution should take place at Dayton, an up-country town between Chattanooga and Knoxville, and that soon afterwards steps for continuing the fight for religious Fundamentalism should take a definite form in the establishment in East Tennessee of Bob Jones College. This institution was started in 1927, with an evangelist's name, strong moral support, and the expressed purpose of holding boys and girls to the spiritual teachings of the fathers. The attendance in time surpassed a thousand, and this was one answer to such outside critics as H. L. Mencken, Clarence Darrow, and others who told the world about Dayton.

The Piedmont country is full of large and small colleges having a Protestant denominational origin, control, or affiliation. These are to be found at Birmingham, Atlanta, Chattanooga, and various smaller centers, including Rome, Georgia, and Greenville, South Carolina. Among these schools the larger denominations have predominated, with Methodist Panthers and Baptist Bulldogs battling annually for local football supremacy at Birmingham. But Presbyterians and others have a foothold. The Congregationalists can claim Piedmont College at Demorest, a Georgia village in the woods on the highway between Atlanta and Asheville, North Carolina. I have heard eloquent sermons on the merits of the church college by small-town preachers whose education did not include a day in any college. They emphasized religious education, character development, and the proportion of our great men who have attended such institutions, sampling the rolls of all the professions for striking examples.

Surpassing the strictly church institutions in many ways as a mission school is the Berry College near Rome. It was founded in 1926 by Martha Berry, who for years earlier had been operating the Berry School for mountain boys and girls. It is a place where young people from the uplands and lowlands of the Southeast can partly pay for tuition and board by working on farms, in dairies, in shops, or in other enterprises which the college operates. The two institutions, school and college, own many thousand acres of land in different counties. This undertaking for the practical education of boys and girls of limited means and opportunity was founded by a native for natives. It became a Tuskegee for whites, and Martha Berry became a Booker T. Washington for mountaineers, receiving financial support from such national figures as Henry Ford and Adolph Ochs. She appealed constructively to the imagination of the up-country when the Ku Klux Klan was riding high, and she utilized the nativistic urge for humanitarian purposes. Her work blended with the mind of the hills.

There are modern methods for advancing the old teachings of frontier religion, and these methods are used in the up-country. Billboards tell tourists about the day of Judgment. Militant groups at Birmingham, Knoxville, and intermediate points have taken to the practice of raising money for fighting the Devil over the radio, and they frequently launch their attacks early in the morning. A large crowd of the faithful put on a vigorous demonstration of protest at Knoxville on an occasion when a broadcasting station withdrew its policy of selling time for such purposes.

The strict adherents of the old-time religion in the hills are in a minority, divided among themselves, and far from consistent in practicing what they preach. As I heard an evangelist say, they may "pray on their knees on Sunday and prey on their neighbors on Monday." They do not apply Christianity systematically to horse-swapping. But their religious beliefs give tone to the social attitudes and practices of the region. Because of these beliefs the rural school-teacher may refrain from going to dances. Beer and movies may not be available on Sundays, and town drugstores may close for the Sunday morning church service. For many years religion prevented women from playing games with cards which men could gamble with. Longer than elsewhere a theatrical performance was regarded in this country as the Devil's workshop.

The religion of the hills continues to stress personal salvation and the institutions of the hills continue to stress individual morality. Individual values clearly predominate over community values, and social responsibilities are only dimly appreciated on the countryside. This was concretely illustrated by the calculations of an Alabama Methodist preacher. Applying both commercial and celestial arithmetic to the statistics of an annual report of the North Alabama Conference of his church, he pointed out to me that circuit-riders, with low pay and large lists of sinners brought into the fold, were saving souls at a per-capita cost about one-tenth of what a few city pastors required. Were those urban shepherds worth their salt? Bishop Warren Candler, the Methodist leader who was for a time head of Emory University in Atlanta, was critical of church emphasis on social service, which, according to his view, meant inadequate attention to the doctrine of spiritual rebirth and adjustment of the individual. Denominational social creeds of modern days have received criticism in the hill country, and Fundamentalists have hit out at the Federal Council of Churches of Christ with twin charges of modernism and radicalism.

The Negro church and clergy surpass the white in centering concern on personal salvation for the next world rather than moving into the problems of the day. They got that way in the era of slavery and have not yet made a wide departure from it. They constitute a bulwark of conservatism and individualism, as H. R. Cayton and George S. Mitchell point out in their study of *Black Workers and the New Unions.*

Most of the lower Piedmont, as a young country with lingering frontier conditions, has had no little consciousness of inferiority. This attitude has characterized individuals and groups. In pre-Civil War times there was recognition of economic, social, and political inferiority to the lowlands, where planter families gave an aristocratic leavening to society. As long as slavery lasted and even later there was a tendency among independent farmers of the up-country to take on certain ways of the planters, with the women in particular seeking to avoid being classed as "poor whites." They might be "planters" only in their own little bailiwick, but such they were. A farmer and storekeeper sometimes called himself on his stationery a "merchant and planter," knowing that he was not one of those aristocrats of the Old South. But there were workers and tenants who were consciously inferior in status to him. The Negro was the last shock-absorber in this scheme of inferiorities and must know his place.

Neither the men nor the women of the up-country ever acquired the leisure or the sense of leisure which has been associated with planter society. By necessity they were more concerned with making a living than with the manner of living. In time they became critical of "broken-down aristocrats" and tended to attach more importance to good individuals than to "good families." After all, it was only "three generations from shirt-sleeves to shirt-sleeves," and in business, as in religion, "every tub has to stand on its own bottom." So ran the doctrine of individualism, which also held that "competition is the life of trade."

The hill country after the Civil War became a land of economic men as it hit its stride with the expansion of agriculture and the coming of industry. In the scheme of thinking, production was more important than consumption, saving was more important than spending, and business was preferable as a career to politics. Successful men seemed to be stingy and hardboiled and even to enjoy jokes about their love of money. Preachers suggested that the Lord loveth a cheerful giver but emphasized that there was a high correlation between this giving and individual prosperity.

Bill Nixon, my father, was an economic man of the hills and would not object to being called one. He was exceptional only as an intensive personification of certain ideas common to his time and region. He learned the value of a dollar by teaching school to save up two hundred and fifty dollars with which to start in business in the middle eighties. Sometimes spending money, by his own confession, was "like cutting eye teeth" for him. Settling down as a merchant and farmer at a new railroad station, he centered attention on money-making as his goal and his game. He seldom let pastime or religion interfere with work or business. He taught his sons that business is a continual fight and that a man will do his best when working for himself rather than for the other fellow. "Better a peanut business of your own than a good salary," he said, and he practiced what he preached. Praise for financial success and for good farming was praise which pleased him most. Conspicuous production or acquisition meant more to him in terms of prestige than conspicuous consumption. He was an individualist seeking by the hardest for all the gain the traffic would bear. Whenever possible he worked side by side with his laborers, especially if wages were high. He set a good pace, and his employees earned their pay. He remarked in later life that he would have had more success out West where rewards were greater for his way of work.

The captain of commerce or industry became the dominant character of the New South, filling the role of the planter of the Old South. This character became the pattern or ideal in the mind of many an aspiring boy of town or country. Industry seemed something to enter and agriculture something to avoid. Farm people came in time to envy the lot of the urban industrialists and entrepreneurs, while the latter might in turn feel dependent on distant financial centers for credit and capital. The hill country now looked northward to the great marts of money and trade rather than southward to the old regions of agrarian life and culture. It consciously became the lower border of the industrial country instead the upper border of the plantation country. It accepted the economic decision of the Civil War and went to work.

This shift in economic life and outlook brought on mixed feelings of optimism and inferiority. Factories and employment seemed good for the region, and the coming of outside capital was nearly always welcome. Tax concessions and other inducements were frequently offered to attract investments. Southern industrial centers could now show high-tariff spokesmen who departed widely from the teachings of John C. Calhoun. Jacob Viner, the economist, wrote in the old *Century* magazine in the winter of 1930 that the "growing industrialization of the Southeast has brought with it the tariff attitudes of the older industrialized areas."

The coming of the twentieth century found the hill country in a national hook-up for economic development. It had put Populistic doctrines further from mind than had portions of the West, and it was cultivating an increasing kinship with Eastern economic orthodoxy. The changing political philosophy of the region in the Coolidge era was aptly described with a bit of exaggeration by the Will Rogers comment that "Yankees are swarming into the South like locusts" and that the "rascals bring their Republican politics with 'em." The industrial and Protestant Piedmont, not the old plantation sections and centers, gave majorities to Hoover over Al Smith in 1928. The new country was not so strongly wedded to the South's political traditions as the old. It had a different brand of conservatism.

The hill country has had critics of its industrial trends. Adolph Ochs and Henry Watterson, two upper South journalists, sounded early warnings of evils of outside control that would result from the Henry Grady formula of bringing in great amounts of industrial investments. Jonathan Daniels, in his book, *A Southerner Discovers the South,* has a chapter on Atlanta as the "Overseer's Capital," noting that agents and viceroys have headquarters there for managing the Southern colonial province for imperial absentee owners.

Social critics have pointed out analogies between absentee ownership of industries and absentee ownership of farm properties in the South. They have emphasized that both interfere with the people's real independence, put them in an inferior status, and perpetuate a colonial economy. This idea ran through the meetings of the Southern Policy Committee in Atlanta and Chattanooga in the middle thirties as well as in subdivisions of that organization. Speaking as one of the leaders of this group at Anniston, Alabama, in 1935, Brooks Hays, who is now in Congress from Little Rock, Arkansas, made an address of unexpected significance. The service clubs and the city's Chamber of Commerce were holding their inter-club summer dinner, and were glad to have him as visiting speaker and other Southern Policy leaders as guests. These guests consisted of three professors, a farm organization officer, and two labor men, George Googe and Steve Nance, of Atlanta. As a summer resident of the county, I had these visitors and Hays at a mountain camp all day before the dinner. We talked about the ills of the South and the way out. We told the speaker what he would be up against with an audience that would be divided in its support or response. He got primed and came down from the mountain like an evangelist carrying the gospel. At the dinner he made a stirring appeal for the South to face the evils of absentee ownership of farms and industries and to give the common man a chance. It was "a challenging address," said the Anniston *Star*. We visitors learned a few days later that the business meeting that followed our pro-

gram and departure was to consider requesting the governor
to send troops to break a strike at a local mill, which New
York owners were threatening to close for good unless there
was favorable action. The proposal was voted down and the
strike issues were settled by other methods. The speech,
delivered without thought or knowledge of the pending
question, was pointed and effective.

The colonial economy theme has occupied the minds of
observers from the Piedmont country to Texas, where Walter
Prescott Webb has explored the subject, particularly in his
Divided We Stand in 1937. An important variation of the
theme is the analysis of Southern manufacturing as to the
value it adds to its raw material or the value of the output
by a unit of labor. The analysis has consistently shown the
region trailing other regions on both counts. Much of its
manufacturing has consisted of the processing or partial
processing of coarse goods, with other sections leading in
turning out finished products of high quality. In this industrial processing the South uses more labor and less machinery
proportionately than the North. This in itself means low
wages in industry, as Clarence Heer and other economists
have pointed out.

That the unfavorable system tends to perpetuate itself
through the region's population increase is implied in the
population studies of Rupert Vance and his colleagues, of
the University of North Carolina. Raise wages to break the
vicious circle, say many New Deal economists and labor
leaders. But lower wages attract new industries, while immediate removal of wage differentials will tend to freeze industrial growth and continue agricultural poverty, according to

the views and writings of economists like John V. Van Sickle, of Vanderbilt University. Discriminatory freight rates on Southern manufactured products are holding the region back, say TVA economists and Southern governors, especially Governor Arnall, who has succeeded in getting a Georgia state case before the Supreme Court on the issue. John L. Lewis, when he was a New Dealer, showed concern for doing something about sharecroppers as essential for a healthy labor movement in the South. His Southern officers took up the issue, supporting farm-tenant legislation. Certain Southerners of the up-country have said simply that more economic opportunity for the Negro would be a remedy for regional poverty. World War II temporarily suspended or reversed a few of the elements in this picture, but it did not solve them. The field is still wide open for critics. The up-country since World War I has manifested several types of regional thinking. One of these centers around Howard W. Odum, the sociologist of the University of North Carolina, whose exhaustive study of *Southern Regions of the United States* appeared in 1936 and foreshadowed the New Deal report on the South as the nation's number one economic problem. Odum, a native of Georgia, had already served on President Hoover's Committee on Social Trends and had taken the lead in organizing a special Southern Regional Committee of the Social Science Research Council.

Another type of regional approach has been carried on by the "Nashville agrarians," who in 1930 brought out *I'll Take My Stand*. In this "Twelve Southerners" dealt with "The South and the Agrarian Tradition." It might be said that the essential chapters were written by men of Middle Tennesee and North Alabama. I myself wrote a middle chapter, "Whither Southern Economy?" In subsequent writings Donald Davidson, of Vanderbilt University, has been the most faithful and consistent spokesman of the "agrarian" school. He has challenged the claims of progress, industrialism, social science, social planning, and most of the ideas or works which might be linked with the New Deal. He attacks the Leviathan of business and of government and warns against giant capitalism as well as giant socialism.

Both Davidson and Odum reflect a strong regional consciousness, the former as a literary man in love with the South's past and fearful of the future, the latter as a social scientist with hopes for a better South in a better nation. Davidson would like to envisage his region largely as an autonomous section, while Odum wishes the region to function in harmony with national trends. The two part company widely in matters of race relations, which Odum faces with sympathy, Davidson with alarm.

The civilization of the Piedmont gets large attention in the symposium, *Culture in the South,* which came from the University of North Carolina Press in 1934 under the editorship of W. T. Couch, its director. Many of the writers were from the hills, though the whole South was covered in various forms. Davidson contributed a chapter, but Couch, in introducing the book, paid severe respects to *I'll Take My Stand* as an unrealistic treatment of the South. The North Carolinian undertook to complete his thought with action, taking an important part in the activities of the Southern Policy Committee and the Southern Conference for Human Welfare.

Lower Piedmont Country

The most formidable of social criticism to come out of the New South is *The Mind of the South,* which appeared in 1941 under the single authorship of W. J. Cash. This Carolina journalist surveyed the currents of thought of the Old South and the New, finding them sadly lacking, partly because of the influence of a violent climate and violent tempers. The whole region has been and is naively unrealistic and uninformed. To the Donald Davidson "agrarians" he gave credit for "puncturing the smugness of Progress," but they over-idealized the Old South and turned their gaze sentimentally backward. He found the industrialists still dominated by a frontier individualism and unwilling to face the facts of modern society. In reviewing his book the "agrarians" gave him no mercy.

Important checks are operating in a positive manner against the regional emphasis or interpretation, whether of the Odum, Davidson, or Cash approach. The labor movement, as the capital movement that preceded it, cuts across regional lines with no idea of pitting section against section. It is cutting across race lines. The concentration of wealth and economic power is not a conspiracy against the South. Whatever conspiracy there may be is against the masses of the North as well as of the South, and Southerners are both members and victims of the conspiracy. The Negro is more and more becoming a Northerner as well as Southerner, and this trend is going to make the South less solid and less separate. Recognition of these anti-regional factors is coming earlier in the Southern up-country than in the low country.

The lower hill country is associated with the writing, contents, and meaning of three important pieces·of fiction which have appeared since 1930. Margaret Mitchell, a native and newspaper feature writer of Atlanta, brought out *Gone With the Wind*, a first novel, in 1936 after years of preparation. It deals with the years of Civil War and Reconstruction, the transition from the Old South to the New, and the decline of the glorified society that was based on slavery. In a long and sustained narrative, the heroine, Scarlett O'Hara, moves from luxury through poverty and back to wealth and security by means of her individual economic tactics that mean the loss of the man she most loves. The book made a national hit as a moving story, rich in detail but not burdened either with sentimentality or social analysis. As a motion picture it was received in Atlanta with a great burst of regional patriotism. Here was the country of *Gone With the Wind* temporarily worshiping the legend of its past, from which it had widely departed.

Erskine Caldwell's *Tobacco Road*, which came out in 1932 and was dramatized for a long run, portrays another type of agrarian decline. Caldwell was born in rural North Georgia not far from Atlanta, attended Erskine College in upper South Carolina, and turned his attention to the ways and doings of poor whites. His *Tobacco Road* country is in the Georgia hinterlands back from the old city of Augusta. Whatever Caldwell's creative imagination did to the novel, the external facts of economic and social decay in this section were strikingly abundant at the beginning of the thirties. It was in a general area where more farm acres were being abandoned than anywhere else in the United States. There were plenty of examples to illustrate the saying by the Bill Arp author that "a sorry farmer on a sorry farm is a sorry sight." It was a natural place to find or create Jeeter Lester and make him a symbol for identifying the poor white in contemporary literature.

Jeeter exemplifies three generations of the decline of man on declining land. He is the final degenerate and dull-witted squatter without a mule or tools. He is unable and unwilling to adjust himself to the changing economic forces. No mill work for him. Farm failure that he is, he nevertheless loves the soil, maybe like a poet or like a mere animal of the woods. With so many things denied to him and his kind, only sex-life is left, and this puts comedy in the tragedy under the naturalistic treatment. Shields McIlwaine wrote in the last sentence of the *Southern Poor-White* that "on Tobacco Road in Georgia, Jeeter Lester reached the dead end of the sharecropper's row." Cash designated Caldwell and William Faulkner as "romantics of the appalling." Hamilton Basso, another Southerner, pronounced *Tobacco Road* "a triumph of distortion and imagination."

This characterization of the "trashy Cracker" put many Southern gentlemen in a dilemma for defense against it. They had too frequently emphasized the thriftlessness and shiftlessness of the poor whites, assuming that there was nothing to do for them but to leave them alone. If *Tobacco Road* was caricature, it was caricature of their own point. Were they ready to surrender their point and move toward social responsibility?

Strange Fruit, which appeared in 1944, is a regional novel dealing with the love of an educated Negro girl for a white man. Its author, Lillian Smith, of an old Southern family, had for some years been living at Clayton, Georgia, north of

Atlanta. Here she and Paula Snelling had established *The North Georgia Review*, later designating it *The South Today*. In this magazine they frankly took up the unfinished business and the unsolved problems of the South, setting forth things to do in the sphere of race relations. They soon had much to say about particular features and applications of the pattern of segregation. Lillian Smith said, "Stop telling 'nigger jokes,'" and, "Use courtesy titles when speaking to educated Negroes or about them." She called for racial justice in labor relations and in the armed forces. She observed that Christianity should mean breaking bread together without a color line. She said that "customs are changing" despite sharp bitter symptoms of reaction, with Gene Talmadge (in common with many prominent business men) trying to exploit the storm while it lasts. She must have had the writing of her own novel in mind in suggesting a little skillful use of shock-therapy on the South.

Strange Fruit was a bestseller and was also dramatized. It shocked many because of its frank treatment of a startling bi-racial theme. It shocked both Southerners and Bostonians, because it seemed coarse in word and implication. Whatever its literary limitations as a first effort, it reflects an insight into the colored mind, into group and personal frustrations. Portraying life in the small-town South, it shows the connection between a lynching and the culture of a whole community.

The hill country is witnessing a substantial amount of criticism of the regional scene. The critics include vanguard spirits of the Lillian Smith type, who are willing to make sweeping changes in certain folkways and to have outside help in bringing on these changes. There are many of a different group, like John Temple Graves, the Birmingham columnist and native of the Coosa country, who wish to make haste slowly without discarding traditions and without outside interference by New Dealers, New Yorkers, the Negro press, or others. They wish the South to be left alone to solve its own problems. Finally, there are many non-critics and critics of the critics. These wish Southerners to be left alone to solve their own problems and then not solve them.

The newspaper press of the Piedmont is less complacent and more alive to social issues than once was the case. That is true, for instance, of the different papers of Atlanta and Birmingham. Southern historians, economists, sociologists, political scientists, and other regional groups have been meeting annually for some years, frequently in Atlanta, to give learned attention to features of Southern society. The groups include social scientists from the staff of TVA, which has made a clear impact on the social outlook of the hill country. Leaders concerned with mass education have come into this picture in search of ways and means for utilizing the fruits of learned research in a popular manner.

Franklin D. Roosevelt touched the popular mind of the hill country in important ways which did not characterize his influence in other sections. His first bid for the presidency stirred memories of Populist days and Bryan days in the back country. His use of the phrase "forgotten man" had a personal meaning to hillbillies, and it carried more significance for them than when used by others, as by William Graham Sumner some decades earlier. He dramatized the statement of Southern problems as no one at Washington had done since the Civil War. As a fighter for his program, he made friends and enemies as well as a deep impression in a region which rather likes to call itself the "Fighting South."

The Squire of Hyde Park had a part-time Georgia home before he was President, before he was governor of the Empire State. He became an adopted citizen of the Empire State of the South, and he enjoyed himself at Warm Springs among the pines, down where the uplands end and the lowlands begin. Southern governors and Southern leaders made pilgrimages for conference with him at the "Little White House" in Georgia. He made speeches up and down the Piedmont, becoming a modern circuit rider and preaching economic salvation. Offended conservatives took up states' rights arguments against him as did their ancestors against Lincoln before the Civil War. Others thought and talked differently. "I tell you," said a construction worker to another on a daycoach coming into Chattanooga, "things are different from the way they were when we were boys, and the government just has to regulate more." Said a rural filling station man between Atlanta and Birmingham in 1937, "Roosevelt has got us all to thinking about the Constitution, and the Constitution has to change with the times." A process of adult education moved through the hills.

It was poetically fitting that the political heir of the South's Jefferson and Jackson should come to the end of his life in his Georgia home. It was impressive for his funeral train to move from one end to the other of the Piedmont country, through the hills where people still believe strongly in the old-time religion. He touched this country in death. Thus passed in a time of crisis the chief who had come to power in a time of crisis one hundred years after the stars fell on Alabama.

Postword

THE MAKINGS of a new mechanical revolution and warnings
of a mass folk movement appeared in the cotton belt while
this book was being written. The base of this development is
in the lowlands but it is spreading to parts of the uplands,
where counter measures are also coming into play to absorb
the shock.

The development comes about directly through the final
successful mechanization of cotton production from the
preparation and planting to the harvesting of the fleecy
staple. After years of expensive research the mechanical
cotton picker is on the job in the Deep South and will soon
become widely available with the removal of wartime restrictions. It was used successfully on several farms in 1945
and 1946. This machine can move along cotton rows and
harvest a bale of cotton at a total cost that is about what
was paid for hand labor for picking a bale back in the low-
wage period around 1896. Paired with this labor-saving de-
vice is the mechanical substitute for the man with the hoe.

Postword

This is an adaptation of the flame-thrower, which moves along with tractor power and destroys weeds and grass but leaves plenty of cotton to grow. Cotton farmers have long had mechanical planters and multiple-plow cultivators. The process is complete for the great planters to tell sharecroppers and a majority of their wage hands to beat it. Many such workers who departed in wartime need not come back.

Hundreds of thousands of sharecroppers, tenants, and small farmers in the main portions of the cotton belt may soon be asking, "Where do we go from here?" In time the number of persons displaced could run into millions. It is true that since time immemorial cotton farming has been carried on by unskilled labor and has been associated with a dense agricultural population as well as with a comparatively low income per capita. The mechanical revolution is converting that situation to one of fewer farmers and workers with higher incomes. The displaced workers, who will include a large proportion of Negroes, are going to seek employment in the hill country and in various other parts of America. They will have to make a flight from cotton in an upheaval as significant as the early Industrial Revolution was for hand weavers and spinners. The reduction of the human factors in cotton culture is piling up human problems for the cotton country and for the nation.

The map of the cotton belt, moreover, will shift, unless government restrictions prevent expansion and government subsidies at the same time save unprofitable areas for the staple. The crop will tend to shift more and more to the great river valleys and the Southwestern plains, where large-scale mechanization is most feasible. Low-cost competition will take cotton away from much of the hill country, continuing a process that became evident in wartime. Only low-cost production or heavy production subsidies can sustain cotton in a world market and permit its use for new or cheap products, such as insulating material and coarse fabrics. It has lost quality uses to rayon and nylon, even in the cotton-mill woman's manner of living.

There will be more green pastures and fine cattle on a thousand hills, with row crops disappearing. Many of the best farmers have been turning to cattle for the past few years with an interest in pure breeds and scientific pasturage. The climate which is good for cotton is also good for cattle, making grazing suitable for most of the months of the year. Bank credit and government aid for that type of farming have become readily available. New farmers and young farmers are learning cattle farming and hay farming and departing from the cotton ways of their ancestors. Some are taking up dairying, which offers opportunities with a growing urban market and with a trend toward correcting the milk deficit in the Southern diet. Other farm changes are being made, such as adding more hogs and poultry. I discovered a small farmer in the Coosa Valley who had ceased losing money on cotton and was making money or a living raising chickens. He was doing all his work alone, growing much of his feed and using one of his two tenant houses as space for incubators and brooders. He was spending much of the night time watching his biddies and reading pulp magazines. The other tenant house was rented for cash. Gone were the tenant families.

These new farm practices do not deplete the soil of plant

food as does cotton. In fact they improve it. They check erosion, which is a patriotic service according to modern prophets and Patrick Henry, who praised gulley-stopping. It is especially needed in this region of sharp slopes, thin soil, and heavy rains.

Many farmers and large landowners are discovering that trees grow fast in the South and that woods mean money, with new possibilities in paper, plywood, and plastics, not to mention the old-line uses for furniture and building material. Scientific forestry and selective cutting are making headway under encouragement by Federal and state forest services. This development sometimes means more income for the landowner, especially for the large one. It is a great act for saving the soil from moving down the creeks and rivers toward the sea. It also contributes to flood control. It is a healthy flight from cotton. But it calls for less labor than cattle-raising, while cattle-raising calls for less labor than the growing of cotton. Peter Drucker in "Exit King Cotton" in *Harper's Magazine* for May, 1946, cites the case of an Atlanta business man who recently turned the whole of an inherited tract into timber, getting an income almost for the first time since possessing it twenty years ago. But six cotton croppers are gone and their cabins have been torn down.

The diversified farms of the uplands and the great mechanized farms of the lowlands are making a more efficient use of manpower. They are getting away from methods that keep workers idle much of the year, as has been too true of the sharecropper system. Under that system, the man worked about 125 days in the year and his mule much less, though the cropper's wife, between field and home, often put in as much time as man and mule together. That large reservoir of labor is being dispensed with.

These far-reaching changes in the South are setting many Southerners to thinking about the future of this region, about the place of the South in the nation, and about a national policy for the South. The cotton interests and cotton congressmen are concerned. The Bureau of Agricultural Economics is exploring the problems, as are research foundations and the National Planning Association. King Cotton is no longer king except in a distinctly limited sense, and the rearrangement of his kingdom is an urgent and tremendous task.

It is important that any national legislation or policy for the South's agriculture take account of the differences between the hill country and the great stretches where the furrow may be a mile long and farming seems a sedentary occupation. The AAA crop control of the nineteen thirties was too uniform in application alike to hill and plain, in laying out cotton acreage quotas without regard to the actual suitability or unsuitability of lands for the crop. It was an emergency measure with benefit payments to achieve scarcity rather than efficiency, and it soon met with more opposition or criticism in Texas than in the Southern Piedmont. There were instances in the early stages of the program in which it checked a wholesome movement by small farmers away from cotton, while large farmers complained that they lacked sufficient quotas to meet the cost of equipment and overhead. There is no necessity to repeat the rigidities, and the repetition would prove unfortunate.

Postword

The green light should be maintained for those farmers, mainly on lowlands and plains, who have the land, capital, and equipment for the efficient production of cotton. Whatever public aid or credit is rendered them should be for making them more efficient producers, not for carrying them as a national burden. In general, they should be supported by other measures than arbitrary price-fixing or subsidies. Their need is for a national policy for the encouragement of foreign trade and the discouragement of domestic monopolies. They need an export market for American cotton or American goods manufactured from cotton or both. They need a market for the purchase of supplies that is approximately in line as to prices with the world market in which they must sell. They have a real stake in world economic stability and have abundant cause to be international-minded. Economic isolation will ruin them or at least restrict them to a minor role.

All the cotton farmers of the Delta or the Great Plains can not be "big shots" operating moving factories in fields. The smaller ones may annex themselves for purposes of mechanization to the great ones, somewhat like vassals in the Feudal Age. Big-scale operators may mechanize and acquire cultivation rights from various small owners or perform services for them on a sort of utility-rate basis. Small farmers in the same community may carry on mechanized farming by owning and operating the giant equipment co-operatively. But these adjustments mean a way of farming not traditional in the South. For various reasons, many farmers of the hills as well as numbers in other sections will fail to make the sweeping changes. These will stubbornly stick to the family-size unit and method of farming. Unless they get a break, they will offer a political cleavage which will not be good for those farmers who wish to do big things. The small farmers may raise a voice surpassing that of the champions of small business.

The best answer to the cry of the small farmers would be an enlarged and improved Farm Security Administration for constructive aid to tenants as well as small owners. Subsidies should be applied on a gradually receding basis to encourage a shift from cotton to types of farming more suitable for small farming in different areas and communities. Patience should be exercised toward the administrative agency, so that it may practice patience with the farmers, for it is hard for a family to quit growing cotton. The change requires both a little capital and a little know-how, and, without these two elements, the farmer just sticks to cotton and goes broke. But with limited funds and no little opposition, the FSA performed wonders before and during the war in advancing diversification and conservation on small farms. Its clients increased production for home use, with less under-consumption than formerly, and they made a large contribution of food for freedom. In the long run, it is clearly to the advantage of the large farm interests that small farmers have this service. The conversion programs for the big fellows and the little fellows should move along together, not in opposition.

It is possible in suitable areas for small farmers of the hill country to go in for more intensive farming than is customary in this section, such as growing vegetables or flowers for market, especially near urban centers. There are successful examples of changes to this way of making a living from the soil. But there are limits to this development and to what an expanded government program can accomplish toward establishing men on the land in this region. Farming should be discouraged rather than stimulated on lands where a good living is impossible. Certain areas should be turned over to forestry. Many families must be released from farming if a Jeeter Lester peasantry is to be avoided. Migrations or new avenues of local employment are the hope.

The hill country has the resources for providing new employment and income in other activities besides its agriculture, textiles, and manufacture of iron and steel. There is the revolution that is taking place in the utilization of timber, of which the region has so much. The uses and demands for cheap electricity can be expanded infinitely more than the uses or demands for cotton. The hill country's actual and potential hydroelectricity, its "white coal," offers the basis for a diversified economic development. This factor has already accounted for a substantial progress, with large and small industries coming into the area in times of peace and war. It has brought aluminum plants into East Tennessee and North Alabama. It has aided rural home and community enterprise in the processing and preservation of food products as well as in other ways.

The improved navigation on the Tennessee, which accompanied the power development, is also an aid to industry, as is indicated by new flour mills, grain elevators, freight terminals, boat shops, and shipyards along the way.

The tourist crop is the leading crop in parts of the up-country. It means hundreds of millions of dollars a year to the Southeast. Unlike cotton, it can be widely expanded and it does not exhaust the soil. The Piedmont lies along or across traffic ways between the region of Florida and the Gulf Coast and the Northern regions of business and industry which furnish people and money for vacations. It has forests, parks, hunting grounds, and scenic lakes, with expanded opportunities for fishing and boating. It has had an inherent interest in outdoor recreation from the days of pioneer hunters to those of Bobby Jones, the Atlanta golfer. It needs a popular understanding of the growing importance of recreation in modern society, in which there is more time and money as well as more necessity for turning from work to play. Providing for recreation includes a wide range of big and little services. It may mean a large tourist hotel, a great excursion cruiser, or a new market for the farm food products. It means opportunity for sale of fishing tackle and fishing bait. There is the "worm ranch" at the town of Savannah, Tennessee, on the Tennessee River. I found near Gadsden a young man who was supplementing his rural income by "boarding" and training bird-dogs for various distant owners. At times this side-line brought in his chief income. He was getting real recreation out of his new way of earning money.

Recreation, in all its ramifications, constitutes a great service industry, and the service business is expanding more rapidly than the production of material necessities. Only through an expansion of services can there ever be an approximation of full employment on a permanent basis. That is something for the leaders, planners, and boosters of the hill country to ponder. They have opportunity to develop an outdoor recreation domain for a larger cash income for employment and for the enrichment of the life of their people.

The recreation business, hydroelectricity, scientific forestry, and diversified farming, constitute a "flow economy," in which a continual replenishment balances outgo. The up-country is in serious need of switching to these "flowing" processes from a traditional emphasis on a "store" economy with its exploitable and exhaustive features. The men of the hills have practiced the "store" economy, not only in mining coal and iron, but in various other ways. They have mined timber resources by completely cutting down great and little tracts at one fell swoop. They have mined land by continual cotton-cropping, without replenishing the soil or checking erosion. In other words, they have, by successive and wasteful stages, sold off and sent away valuable stored-up plant food. Most of the region's income and income concepts to date have been based on an exploitable "store" economy. It is time for a change, for a modification of the economic folkways, if there is to be a basis for the good life.

The masses of the Southern hills and plains need a vast amount of what might be called resource education, if the people of this region are to negotiate a successful change to a high-class "flow" economy. That type of education concerns itself with the region's resources, physical and human, and with ways of conserving and harnessing those resources so as to lift the region's level of production, income, and consumption, or whole manner of living. It includes research and investigative study of the region and its problems on a wide range, scientific, economic, and cultural. It also means turning the results of such study into popular understanding and ultimately into wholesome action. It means applied education upward, downward, and outward through schools, extension services, press, radio, and other agencies. Education has an important role to play in utilizing the wartime gains which came to this region in the form of new capital, new technology, and new labor skills. It has a role to play in adjusting people to these new forces.

The greatest problem of the South is that of people, "all these people." Human beings were the South's greatest liability to the nation in the Great Depression, the South's greatest asset to the nation in World War II. In spite of the significant industrial expansion, the Southeast showed a net migration of civilians to other regions between 1940 and the end of 1943, as indicated by ration-book data. There are normally far too many people in the South for the prevailing economy and institutions. This fact helps explain the low income per capita and the limited funds for schools in proportion to the number of children. The large proportion of children seems to cause poverty, and the poverty seems to lead to more children, for the highest birth rate is among the rural poor.

The urban areas of the hill country are between two population pressures. There is the Negro surplus in the black belt, as already mentioned. The rural areas of the Appalachian Mountains have a white population with the most rapid natural increase to be found in America. There is not enough agricultural land, good or poor, to accommodate this increase, and mountaineers need to leave the small farms, while the Negroes are leaving the large ones. They moved away in the twenties, were pushed back or held back in the early thirties, and formed an outward stream again as war ushered in the forties. These changes really constituted great folk movements of Americans seeking a bit of economic security or opportunity. Many of the participants in such movements are rootless and often have faces that register little hope of destination or opportunity as they move about the country in a makeshift manner. This has been strikingly true in hard times, as in the case of a mountain family I once saw making way on the road with the man moving a few belongings and little children along in a handcart. They were frustrated in a land of beauty.

The net export of population to other regions is an economic and institutional strain, whether the migrants be chiefly whites from the hills or Negroes from the black belt. A good proportion of those who go are of an active working age, for the employers are not looking for children or the aged. It costs something to rear these workers from birth and provide them with schooling. The cost falls on families, communities, and states, and it runs into a total of billions for the past thirty years. In return, migrants contribute little or nothing directly to the native communities. Some of them send a little money back, while some take funds away in different ways. The whole procedure is a telling item in the South's unbalanced budget, regardless of how or why it was brought about. It is a differential against the South, though it has not been attributed to a Yankee conspiracy. In simple terms, the South's present economy is not adequate to continue thus to supply the nation with a population reserve.

The population pressure, with its mass shifting, is also disturbing to Southern civic life. It causes the voting to be less. It drags talents of leadership out of towns and rural areas and out of the South. It pushes a large proportion of workers outside the pale of regular employment and social security. It intensifies racial friction when jobs are scarce or when public accommodations are limited.

The hill country needs fewer people or more real income for real people. That is as clear as arithmetic. One answer is migration, which may be unfortunate in its effects both for the South and for the North. Another is a reduction of the birth rate, which is slowly taking place. But this is a long-run remedy and can not meet the issue in our time. The best solution is for the region to produce and consume more goods and services. The Piedmont country can produce more milk and drink it, more meat and eat it, and more clothing and wear it without disturbing the market for any other group or section. It can provide more houses and live in them without taking shelter away from other people. With a broader and higher production base, it can provide more or better facilities for material, professional, and cultural services and use them without causing any readjustment in the national economy. Such a regional progress adds to national progress.

The Southern hill country has a geographical distribution of people and physical resources that is suitable for a decentralized and diversified economic development. That type of development facilitates social stability and fits into a healthy trend away from the massive concentration of industries and workers in abnormal centers. On the negative side, it permits greater security from destruction by the methods of modern warfare. On the positive side, it permits a more natural way of living with more outdoor space for the common man. The pattern of congestion for industry, people, and government came in with the age of steam, and it is no longer necessary in the age of electricity, which does not have to be applied at the point of production. These new possibilities and desirabilities are surveyed by several writers, including the author, in a recent book, *Cities Are Abnormal*. It is feasible for the industrial Piedmont, with so much of its development awaiting the future, to turn from the old trend to the new. This requires a certain amount of foresight and planning, for the South must plan or perish.

The hill country is moving into new frontiers of industrial society as well as of scientific agriculture. In a few months after victory over Japan the establishment of new paper mills to use Southern timber was announced, and a merger wave hit the up-country textile industry, with fabulous sums being paid by absentee owners. The expanded drives by CIO and AFL forces to unionize Southern workers matched this new movement of capital below the Potomac, and the organizers gave plenty of attention to the textile field. Southern workers are joining big unions while Southern industrialists are playing ball with big corporations. Acceptance of the high wage trend is becoming wider. This view was put in pointed terms by a newspaper of the Piedmont, the Greensboro, North Carolina, *News,* which was quoted by a labor journal in May, 1946, as saying, "We are in for a high wage economy, necessarily so; and, in our considered opinion, no section is going to gain as much therefrom as the South." The excerpt continued, "If the Southern states with their manifold advantages can not stand up on an equalized wage scale, then something is sadly wrong with our leadership and the quality of Southern businessmen and industrial management."

The South's colonial economy complex has entered the picture as an argument for unionization and higher wages to prevent absentee owners from exploiting the workers and the region. The CIO particularly has played up this point and circularized the statement that "the very companies which deal with unions in the North all too often try to keep the people below the Mason-Dixon line from organizing and winning the right to bargain collectively."

There are strong Southern complaints about the impersonal movement of capital into the South and the conscious campaign of organized labor which accompanies it. But denunciation of the operating forces will hardly stop them. Maybe they should not be stopped, since the whole process foreshadows more needed capital, greater production, and higher payrolls for the South. But public attention is necessary to guard against financial buccaneering and to prevent monopolistic practices that would injure small business as well as consumers. As in the case of farming, it is important that big and little operators function in coordination, not in opposition.

The South needs an equivalent of the Farm Security Administration for small business and perhaps for small towns, especially to provide types of technical assistance and information based on expert research. For this purpose, small business should include the one-man or family-size units of enterprise. The TVA has provided such assistance through research in ways of processing clays, foods, and other local products. In this it has aided in resource development. In addition to contracts with municipalities for the use of electric power, it has aided lake-front communities in rearranging public properties and services and in laying out new parks. Assistance of this nature should be expanded for the benefit of individuals, groups, and communities.

Since the war bills have been introduced in both houses of Congress to provide for the encouragement of rural industries in backward and suitable areas. The Secretary of Commerce and the Secretary of Agriculture, whose departments would be concerned, are quoted as being in support of this step, as also are the National Grange and the Farmers' Union. With judicious study, planning, and administration, such a program could be made a constructive force in balancing up the economic life, improving the living standards, and developing human skills in the rural South. It would stimulate agricultural diversification in the hill country by providing processing centers for farm products. It might be made more important for its informational and scientific service than for financial aid, which could be put on a sound investment basis. It would make a mass exodus of workers less necessary and also improve the earning power of those going out from their localities. It would clearly in many cases be a factor in conserving the community as a community and thus meeting one of the greatest needs of the rural areas. To achieve this result, there should be a maximum reliance on local and state initiative, as is the general policy of TVA in such matters. That is one way to recapture something of the cooperative spirit of pioneer times, when good neighbors got together for house-raisings, logrollings, road work, and the like.

The up-country, in the economic life of its people, ranks high in the proportion of small farmers, small shopkeepers, and, small craftsmen. The security of these groups may be threatened by the cult of bigness on the industrial front, unless their role is recognized and respected by the great powers-that-be in government, business, and labor. These individuals of the hills crave opportunity. They resent rigid controls of their little affairs, and their moonshine belt has been discovered by OPA administrators as well as by internal revenue officers.

The restless Americans of the Southeastern hills are being studied and surveyed at home and abroad. The most thorough study of the nation's human resources in the South is Vance's *All These People,* which appeared in 1946 and, like Gray's *Elegy,* was seven years in the writing. It is a masterly analysis of a region which has so many children that it is like the old woman who lived in a shoe. It emphasizes this great population reserve as a matter of vital concern both to the South and to the North, and suggests, that, if the United States in the future is going to need and utilize this reserve it should seek a constructive national policy for the South. In other words, the nation should give wise attention to its human seedbed, both as to the amount and the quality of the crop. Vance, like Odum, sees the South as a great testing field for regional-national planning.

The up-country, like the rest of the South, needs more treatment than just being studied as it passes more fully into the ways of a monetary economy for all. It needs plans or policies of action for pulling its standards of production and living up toward the national level. With an eye to progress, important interests are concerning themselves with these matters. These interests embrace banking, industry, farming, labor, education, and religion. They cut across race lines. In Atlanta, more than elsewhere, progress has been made in steps for compounding these various interests. In the halls of Atlanta University, Southern whites and Negroes have frequently met for the mutual consideration of common problems. Outstanding capitalists and labor leaders have appeared together on forum programs at Emory University for the discussion of labor relations in industry. A significant Fact Finding Movement was started in Atlanta before World War II, mainly through the initiative of Josephine Wilkins and other leaders of the local League of Women Voters. With the cooperation of the University of Georgia and the various service clubs of the state, this organization explored the facts of Georgia's industry, agriculture, schools, legislative set-up, prison conditions, and so on. Governor Arnall followed suit by creating a development board composed of leaders representing different economic interests, with active participation by educators. The Georgia capital may become the regional center for making a revision and democratic application of the industrial teachings of Henry W. Grady.

Labor groups and small business interests of the hill country have given strong support to the Southern Governors' Conference in the long contest for lower freight rates for Southern shippers of finished products. These groups, including the governors, were far from agreement, however, on issues of labor standards and minimum wages as well as other matters.

The task of properly evaluating the role of the hill country in the South and the place of the South in the nation would require the service of a body comparable to a British Royal Commission or the National Monetary Commission which prepared the way for the establishment of the Federal Reserve Banks by Congress. It should be concerned with such problems as wage rates, freight rates, cotton policy, and the proposed application of the TVA pattern to other rivers like the Coosa-Alabama system. It should explore the feasibility of projects for housing industrial workers in near-by rural homes with gardens and small farms, so that they may have "one foot on the soil." It should take up other factors of population and income, including regional needs for Federal aid to education and the future of the Negro. It should consider all these subjects in relationship and pull together the findings of various private groups and government agencies, such as TVA, the Bureau of Agricultural Economics, the National Resources Planning Board, the Atlanta Reserve Bank, and the planning commissions of the Southern states. Finally, it should make recommendations of policy with a view to translating thought into action. The work, in part, should be designed to save the New South from the known evils of the Industrial Revolution of earlier times in England and America.

The hill country, however, is something more than a collection of problems. It is not extensively problem conscious, less so perhaps than the deeper portions of the cotton belt. It is a land of promise with its hopes of industrial expansion. It is also a land of variety, where in wartime I have seen farmers using three kinds of power for plowing: tractor, mule, and ox. It has districts where rural shoppers go to town in wagons, buggies, and automobiles. For heating homes hill people are using pine knots, oak wood, coal, oil, gas, and electricity. Some of their women beat wartime shoe rationing by going barefooted in summer. All over the region men hunt for quail, doves, squirrels, rabbits, and possums, and chase foxes. In East Tennessee they sometimes kill a wild boar. The Outdoor Writers of America, in convention assembled at Chattanooga in the spring of 1946, sat down to a banquet and dined on boar meat. Speaking of another sport, a Coosa Valley man says, "We don't worry when we get broke. We just go fishing."

The leading cities of the hills have imported grand opera stars from New York and have had conventions of Sacred Harp singers. The Alabama town of Guntersville, modernized by a TVA lake, nevertheless remains a singing center for the Sand Mountain country. The only problems it had were traffic problems when thousands gathered in and around its courthouse on Sunday, May 26, 1946, for the first unlimited annual meeting for all-day singing after World War II. Local fiddlers may still be heard in the region, while thousands get hillbilly music over the radio. The hill country is a land with

> *New things and old things co-twisted*
> *as if Time*
> *Were nothing. . . .*

Book Notes

THE Lower Piedmont Country as a distinctive region has received little treatment by the writers of books. It has been largely neglected or handled as part of the South along with the lowlands and mountains. Outside the realm of fiction, I have made use of a few works, which might be classed as up-country books. One of these is Hughes Reynolds' study of history and legend, *The Coosa River Valley from De Soto to Hydroelectric Power* (Cynthiana, Kentucky, 1944). Another is Ethel Armes' work, *The Story of Coal and Iron in Alabama* (Birmingham, 1910). This was sponsored by the Birmingham Chamber of Commerce, and it neglects twentieth-century labor issues and problems, which are pointedly treated in a chapter on Birmingham by George Leighton in his *America's Growing Pains: The Romance, Comedy and Tragedy of Five Great Cities* (New York and London, 1939). The greatest up-country editor and publicist is portrayed by Raymond B. Nixon in *Henry W. Grady: Spokesman of the New South* (New York, 1943). My own *Possum Trot* (Nor-

man, Oklahoma, 1941) is the story of a rural community of
the uplands. The singing ways of the region are interpreted
by George P. Jackson in his *White Spirituals of the Southern
Uplands* (Chapel Hill, 1933) and *The Story of the Sacred
Harp* (Nashville, 1944). There is a real need for a good
biography of Sam Jones, the "mountain evangelist," though
there is much by him or about him in out-of-print books.
I have used *Sermons and Sayings by the Rev. Sam P. Jones
of the North Georgia Conference,* edited by W. M. Leftwich
(Nashville, 1885).

If one can not get Bill Arp's *From the Uncivil War to
Date, 1861-1903* (Atlanta, 1903) or other writings by this
North Georgia humorist (Charles H. Smith), the next best
material on him is to be found in Shields McIlwaine's *The
Southern Poor-White from Lubberland to Tobacco Road*
(Norman, Oklahoma, 1939). McIlwaine's study of the place
of Southern poor whites and other non-aristocrats in litera-
ture is also helpful for its nineteen pages of bibliography.

Several state accounts are valuable for light on the political
and social history of the hill country. Among these are
Blanche H. Clark's *Tennessee Yeomen, 1840-1860* (Nashville,
1942), A. M. Arnett's *The Populist Movement in Georgia*
(New York, 1922), C. B. Gosnell's *Government and Politics
of Georgia* (New York, 1936), W. L. Fleming's *The Civil
War and Reconstruction in Alabama* (New York, 1905), H.
M. Bond's *Negro Education in Alabama* (Washington, 1939),
and A. B. Moore's *History of Alabama* (University, Alabama,
1934). Moore made extensive use of newspaper material on
political conflicts between North Alabama and the black
belt. Bond, an able Negro scholar, gives a clear analysis of

social, economic, and political conditions as affecting education in Alabama after the Civil War.

The impact of the TVA development on the life of a large part of the Piedmont country has been surveyed by a number of writers. Mention might be made of David Lilienthal's *TVA-Democracy on the March* (New York, 1944), R. L. Duffus', *The Valley and Its People* (New York, 1944), and Willson Whitman's *God's Valley: People and Power Along the Tennessee River* (New York, 1939).

First-hand observation of conditions around Piedmont cotton mills is presented by J. J. Rhyne in *Some Southern Cotton Mill Workers and Their Villages* (Chapel Hill, 1930) and by Liston Pope in *Mill Hands and Preachers* (New Haven, 1942). Another phase of life in uplands and lowlands is given by Thomas D. Clark in *Pills, Petticoats and Plows: The Southern Country Store,* (Indianapolis and New York, 1944), which covers the period from 1865 to 1915 and is based on a vast amount of original records, letters, and account books. Arthur F. Raper and Ira De A. Reid analyze what they call "modern American feudalism" in *Sharecroppers All* (Chapel Hill, 1941).

The geographic factors of the Piedmont region are ably set forth by Rupert B. Vance in *Human Geography of the South* (Chapel Hill, 1932). The same author's *All These People: The Nation's Human Resources in the South* (Chapel Hill, 1946) is the definitive study of the whole Southern region in terms of population and geography.

These suggested offerings might be expanded with the following list, which includes several books cited in preceding chapters.

Book Notes

Alabama Policy Bulletin No. 14, *Democracy and the Constitution* (Montgomery, 1945).

Byrd, Sam, *Small Town South* (Boston, 1942).

Carmer, Carl, *Stars Fell on Alabama* (New York, 1934).

Cash, W. J., *The Mind of the South* (New York, 1941).

Cason, Clarence, *90° in the Shade* (Chapel Hill, 1935).

Couch, W. T., editor, *Culture in the South* (Chapel Hill, 1934).

Dabney, Virginius, *Below the Potomac* (New York, 1942).

Daniels, Jonathan, *A Southerner Discovers the South* (New York, 1938).

Davidson, Donald, and others, *I'll Take My Stand* (New York, 1930).

Farmer, Hallie, *The Legislative Process in Alabama: Legislative Apportionment* (University, Alabama, 1944).

Federal Writers' Project, *These Are Our Lives* (Chapel Hill, 1939).

Graves, J. T., *The Fighting South* (New York, 1943).

Heer, Clarence, *Income and Wages in the South* (Chapel Hill, 1930).

Horn, S. F., *Invisible Empire: The Story of the Ku Klux Klan, 1866-1871* (Boston, 1939).

Johnson, C. S., *Statistical Atlas* (Chapel Hill, 1941).

Johnson, G. W., *The Wasted Land* (Chapel Hill, 1937).

Lomax, J. A. and Lomax, Alan, *American Ballads and Folk Songs* (New York, 1934).

National Emergency Council, *Report to the President on Economic Conditions in the South* (Washington, 1938).

Nixon, H. C., *Forty Acres and Steel Mules* (Chapel Hill, 1938).

Odum, H. W., *Race and Rumors of Race* (Chapel Hill, 1943).

Odum, H. W., *Southern Regions of the United States* (Chapel Hill, 1936).

Raper, Arthur F., *Tenants of the Almighty* (New York, 1943).

Robertson, Ben, *Red Hills and Cotton* (New York, 1942).

Van Sickle, J. V., *Planning for the South* (Nashville, 1943).

Index

Index

240

Index

Index

Index

Index